UPGRADE YOUR MINDSET

How to overcome limiting beliefs and tap your potential

VINITA BANSAL

CONTENTS

INTRODUCTION	1
CHAPTER 1: Mindset Matters	9
Fixed Mindset is Limiting	11
Growth Mindset is Freedom	13
Leading With a False Growth Mindset	16
What's Your Mindset?	22
CHAPTER 2: Start With Brain	33
First: Step Into the Arena	35
Second: Change the Way You Talk to Yourself	39
Third: Shape Your Identity	46
Fourth: Imitate the People You Admire	53
Finally: Mix it to Fix it	57
CHAPTER 3: Get Comfortable With Mistakes	65
Destigmatize Mistakes: Nobody is Perfect	72
Break it Down: What's Under Your Control	77
Recognize Negativity: Denial and Self-Justification	81
Reframe Reality: Letting Go and Owning Up	86
Remind Yourself: You Aren't Alone	91
CHAPTER 4: Apply Incredible Power of Yet	97
Is There Something You Can't Do Yet?	101
Try it One More Time	104
Ask for Help	111
Face Your Critics	118

See How Far You Have Come	124
CHAPTER 5: Invest in the Right Kind of Effort	**129**
Think Long Term	134
Recombine Ideas	139
Seek the Right Level of Difficulty	144
Turn Intent to Action	150
CHAPTER 6: Build Emotional Resilience	**159**
What's Holding You Back?	165
Failure is Part of the Process	171
To Succeed Forget Self-Esteem	175
CHAPTER 7: Craft Your Vision	**183**
Goal Setting	189
Fear Setting	197
Climbing the Mountain	202
Bridging the Gap	211
Mindset Tracker	**215**
BONUS: Promoting Growth Mindset in Kids	**219**
Conclusion	221
About the Author	225
What to read Next?	226
Notes	229

INTRODUCTION

ON OCTOBER 31, 2003, Bethany Hamilton, aged 13 at the time, went for a morning surf along Tunnels Beach, Kauai in Hawaii, with her best friend Alana Blanchard, Alana's father and brother, when a 14-foot-long tiger shark attacked her. She was rushed to the hospital only to discover later that she lost 60 percent of the blood in her body, and most of her left arm was gone. For most people, this would have been an end to their surfing career. But not for Bethany. Just four weeks after the attack, Bethany was back on her board surfing again and within two years she won her first national surfing title.[1]

Bethany looked past setbacks, overcame some of the hardest challenges, and pursued her goals to build the life she desired for herself. She did not let a drastic event in her life define who she was. Rather, she poured all her energy into becoming the person she wanted to be. In her book *Soul Surfer*, she writes, "Life is a lot like surfing... When you get caught in the impact zone, you've got to just get back up. Because you never know what may be over the next wave."[2]

Katharine Graham's life changed abruptly when her husband committed suicide in 1963 and she was left to take charge of "The Washington Post." She had been a socialite and a housewife all her life and had no experience running a business. With no real-world experience in leading a company and a struggling newspaper, the odds were not in her favor. While many expected her to sell the company, she decided to run it herself. As the only woman to be in such a high position at a publishing company, she had no female role models and had difficulty being taken seriously by many of her male colleagues and employees.[3]

Despite the overwhelming number of obstacles and disadvantages she faced, she continued in her efforts to study everything intensely. She went on a journey of personal transformation, chose a path of learning and growth and with the help of friends and many others, gained confidence and acquired the skills that enabled her to transform "The Washington Post" into one of the leading newspapers in the United States. From a reluctant inexperienced leader, she went on to become a highly successful and respected one. It was her effort and perseverance and not her experience or skills that made her one of the most successful and admired business leaders of her time. Under her leadership, the paper provided readers with courageous and award-winning editorial coverage of controversial issues such as the Watergate scandal and the Pentagon papers.

These words summed up her life in so many ways "She was gutsy, so many said, yet never trumpeted the fact. Her wealth and influence were great, but wielded with grace. She changed the course of the nation, her city and journalism, and in so doing knocked down walls for women."[4]

Josh Waitzkin caught his first glimpse of chess while he was walking with his mother in New York City's Washington Square Park at the age of 6. He fell in love with the game and became an international master and the U.S. Junior Co-Champion by the time he was 16. When he was 21 years old, he began to transition away from chess into the study of Chinese martial art, Tai Chi Chuan, and became a champion there as well.

While many would call Waitzkin "gifted," he credits his success to the learning process by which he developed those skills. He said "I learned so much from the game. And you know, more than anything, chess for me was a channel for internal growth. I loved learning from the game, learning about life, learning about myself, learning about how I reacted to different situations. What I love from chess, about chess, was that pure, pure relationship to the game."[5]

He won many games and enjoyed those wins, but he did not consider those events as the defining moments of his life. What propelled him to success wasn't those wins, but the lessons that he learned from his losses. What kept him going despite the pain of defeat was the long-term perspective and his ability to consider those defeats as opportunities for growth. He said, "loss was ultimately, maybe the most important thing that's ever happened to me in my competitive career, because it taught me first of all that the road to winning isn't about innate talent or about perfection, but it's about overcoming adversity, about rebounding from defeat."[6]

What do Bethany Hamilton, Katharine Graham, Josh Waitzkin and many other highly accomplished and successful people have in common?

Yes, it was their effort, resilience, determination, and love for learning that got them successful. But, what created them all was their mindset. Their mindset was critical to their success. It was their mindset that prevented setbacks from defining or destroying them. It was their mindset that turned each challenge into a critical lesson. It was their mindset that encouraged them to build the skills they needed to be successful in their goals. It was their mindset that created a passion for learning more than the passion for winning.

Some of the most accomplished and successful people like Walt Disney, Steven Spielberg, Einstein, and J.K. Rowling were initially regarded as people without a future. But they went on to achieve success by building their abilities and putting in the effort. From barely surviving to actually thriving, what guided them all along was their mindset. They failed repeatedly, but got up each time and kept going. They didn't admit defeat. They didn't call it quits or head for the ropes.

We all face challenges in life. Each challenge is an experience that teaches us a critical lesson: what's important in those moments when we face a setback, when things don't go our way, or when everything seems to fall apart is our mindset. Instead of letting obstacles be the reason for our failure, we can turn them around by considering them as opportunities for growth. We can build the life we wish for ourselves only if we learn to face our fears, fight our inner critic and put our effort into building the right skills.

People who see every mistake as a crisis, or every failure as a sign that they are losers, stop taking risks, become less creative, and avoid challenges. They essentially stop learning anything new. They are so focused on the final outcome that they stop paying attention to their learning in the process.

To fulfill your potential, you have to start thinking differently. You have to believe that you are not limited by your current capabilities. By changing your ability to think right, you can change your ability to perform. You can bring your game to an entirely new level.

HOW THIS BOOK WILL BENEFIT YOU

This book is a culmination of my years of thinking and practice into words. Every single day practicing the right mindset helps me be a better version of myself. It has helped me fulfill my potential and I hope the strategies in this book help you fulfill your potential too.

I used to call it a force, mystical power, some sort of a feeling until Carol Dweck, a Stanford University psychologist popularized the word mindsets with her research back in 2007. When I first read about the power of two mindsets - fixed mindset and growth mindset - I immediately knew that what I had been calling my force all along was nothing but my mindset. With better terminology, her research, and the work of multiple other researchers, I started creating a plan for developing a growth mindset. This book encompasses my life experience - everything I learned by putting these methods into practice. There wasn't a single defining moment or an event in my life that changed my mindset. It has been a gradual process of experimenting, observing, refining and learning. *Upgrade Your Mindset* is all about that process.

In this book, you will learn how even a small change in mindset can have a tremendous impact on how you make decisions, act, and ultimately the life you lead. I draw knowledge and research from neuroscience, philosophy, psychology, and many other fields that have been around for many years and connect them together in ways that are easy to understand and apply in real life. You will find practical advice to separate helpful from unhelpful behaviors, understand why some things work and others do not, and take back control of your life with the realization that each one of us have supreme power over the choices we make. You aren't born to be a certain way. You can be the architect of your own life.

Ten key ideas you will find in this book:

1. Overcome limiting beliefs to tap into your potential.
2. Let go of negative self-talk and reframe it with a more positive tone.
3. Shape your identity to redefine who you are in the world.
4. Shift from denying or justifying to accepting mistakes to help you grow.
5. Achieve better results with the vision and motivation to improve in the future.
6. Let go of fear and self-doubt to lead with courage and possibilities.
7. Invest in the right kind of effort instead of working incredibly hard and not moving forward.
8. Get back on track when you get off-course with challenges and setbacks.
9. Stay real by cultivating self-compassion instead of chasing after high self-esteem.
10. Craft your vision and plan of action to achieve your goals and bridge the gap.

By practicing these 10 key ideas, your actions will work for you instead of against you. As you take this personal journey of transformation, your mindset will not only bring positive changes in your life, but those around you will feel the difference too. You will stop comparing yourself to others and start competing with self because you will feel empowered to build the life you desire.

Additionally, you will:

- Establish a deeper understanding of how mindset works.
- Take steps to recognize your predominant mindset.

- Learn to build a growth mindset in a methodical, systematic way, with practical exercises. The book contains 19 printable downloads with guided exercises to help you put your learning into practice.
- Promote growth mindset in kids with the help of a bonus chapter along with additional resources for cultivating this mindset in kids.

Templates and other resources in this book can be downloaded at: techtello.com/upgrade-your-mindset/templates/

CHAPTER 1

Mindset Matters

YOUR BELIEFS, conscious or unconscious, determine how you think, what you feel, how you act and greatly impact whether you succeed in leading the life you want. [1]

Mindsets are nothing but beliefs. When you aren't able to do something, do you think of it as a limitation of your abilities or an opportunity to embrace new challenges? When you make mistakes, do you spend time criticizing yourself and let those emotions paralyze you or use them to fuel your growth? When you look at successful people, do you think they are more gifted than others, they have talent, their innate abilities made them successful, or do you believe success comes from hard work. Do you invest in building skills by putting in the required effort, trying new strategies, and drawing inspiration from others or do you think it should all come to you naturally?

Stanford University psychologist Carol Dweck's research on the power of mindsets greatly influenced how we think about talent and abilities. She has written about the consequences of thinking that your intelligence or personality is something that you can develop, as opposed to something that is a fixed, deep-seated trait. She said "The view you adopt for yourself profoundly affects the way you lead your life. It can determine whether you become the person you want to be and whether you accomplish the things you value."[2]

What you believe is what you achieve. How you choose to interpret your experiences can set the boundaries on what you can accomplish. When you believe that intelligence and personality is fixed and no amount of effort can enhance it, you give up too soon or refuse to even try. However, when you believe it's something that can be developed, you push ahead with the desire to learn, look at failures and setbacks as a medium for growth, bounce back from challenging circumstances and break the mental barrier to explore new possibilities that didn't seem possible earlier.

Using the right mindset does not guarantee your version of success as it only helps you see the right direction. You still need to take the journey. You may not become the next best writer, climb the list of top ten CEOs, gain the badge of a unicorn startup, earn a Michelin star for your restaurant, win an Olympic medal, or anything else your heart desires. But with the right mindset, you can become a better version of yourself. Your mindset can help you realize your unexplored potential, see opportunities beyond obstacles, and urge you to put in the effort to create your own path to success as opposed to feeling limited by your current abilities.

You can either choose a mindset that limits you by believing in fixed abilities, intelligence, and potential or a mindset that believes you can change, learn and grow through effort, practice and persistence. Which mindset you choose is your decision. Your beliefs are a creation of your mind and you can change them.[3]

FIXED MINDSET IS LIMITING

A person with a fixed mindset believes that people are born with special talents and every person has different abilities and intelligence that cannot get better with time, effort, and determination. They admire successful people for their intelligence and praise them for their talent while refusing to look at the effort and hard work that went into their making behind the scenes. They think of J.K. Rowling, Theodor Seuss Geisel, Albert Einstein, Benjamin Franklin, Stephen King, Oprah Winfrey, Thomas Edison, Michael Jordan, and Walt Disney as popular names around the world due to their innate talent and not a result of their ability to live through failure and persist in their efforts.

Success and failure is a part of their identity.[4] Success means they are smart and talented and failure means they are not. Everything is about the outcome, a direct measure of their competence and worth. Every failure is a validation of their lack of intelligence and every mistake is a reflection of their limitations. Lost a match? They must be terrible at the game. Failed to land a key pitch? They must be stupid. Bombed a presentation? They must not be smart. Failed to deliver a project? All their effort is useless. Didn't get a promotion? They are a loser.

People with a fixed mindset are more concerned with proving they are smart as opposed to learning something new. Instead of making an effort to build new skills, they choose to hide their shortcomings. In their world, saying "I don't know" or asking for help signifies they are less competent. Instead of engaging in constructive criticism and seeking diverse opinions, they favor people who bolster their ego and reinforce their self-esteem. Every disagreement is an attack on their identity. Why would they care about doing the right thing, when all their energy is spent on being right?

No wonder, they refuse to step outside their comfort zone and stick to the known with fear of failure. They are quick to lose interest when things get challenging and often use phrases like - *"It's not for me!" "I can't do it!" "It's better to stick to what I know!" "I am who I am!" "I do not have the ability!" "I give up!" "I can't learn!"* The mindset that they cannot learn and improve limits them.

A fixed mindset[5] tells them to:

- Avoid challenges
- Give up easily
- Believe their abilities cannot be developed
- Worry about how they will be judged
- Run from mistakes and ignore them
- Avoid new expcricnccs with fear of failure
- Look for people who can reinforce their self-esteem
- Blame others for their failures
- Focus only on the outcome as it defines them
- Feel threatened by the success of others
- Ignore negative feedback even though it's useful

PEOPLE WITH A FIXED MINDSET

Run from mistakes	Reinforce self esteem
Blame others	Give up easily
Feel threatened by others success	Avoid challenges
Ignore feedback	Believe talent is fixed

GROWTH MINDSET IS FREEDOM

A person with a growth mindset understands that certain people have special talents and that intelligence varies from person to person, but it's also something that can be developed and increased with effort and hard work. They believe talent is not all there is to achievement as having a talent for something is different from excelling in it. Why think of talent as destiny when there's merit in considering the importance of effort in shaping the person's future?[6]

They also admire successful people, not for who they are, but for what they do. It's the hard work and determination behind the success that's a source of their inspiration. While describing a growth mindset, Carol Dweck said "Even geniuses have to work hard for their achievements. And what's so heroic, they would say, about having a gift? They may appreciate endowment, but they admire effort, for no matter what your ability is, effort is what ignites that ability and turns it into accomplishment."[7]

They do feel bad, even frustrated at times when they fail or make mistakes. But failure doesn't define them. Struggles and setbacks are an opportunity to embrace challenges, reach for their potential and build new skills. Instead of lamenting about their failures, they focus on what to do next. They try to figure out what they have done wrong, what they need to do differently, and when they need to ask for help. Failed a marketing campaign? Try new strategies. Struggling to solve a problem? Work harder. Lost a deal? Create a better sales pitch. Missed a deadline? Build estimation skills.

People with a growth mindset orient towards learning. When they don't know something, they express their ignorance and seek opinions to build a better viewpoint. When they don't have the required skills to complete a task, they stretch themselves to build new skills. When they aren't able to make progress, they do not hesitate to reach out for help. Not knowing something is not a measure of their worth, it's an opportunity to grow. This mindset makes them surround themselves with people who challenge them, who are better than they are, who inspire, nudge and push ahead to the possibilities of a better future.

Growth mindset enables them to embrace challenges without fear of failure. They take joy in the learning process. Things get interesting when they get challenging as it's the moment to try different strategies, dive into new information, push themselves, expand their skills and take constructive action. Growth drives their thinking and they often use phrases like - *"I want to try and not give up!" "I can do it!" "I want to explore new ideas!" "I can learn from my mistakes!" "I just don't know yet!" "I can do better!" "I believe in myself!" "It's ok to fail!"*

A growth mindset[8] tells them to:

- Accept challenges
- Persevere in the face of failures and setbacks
- Believe in growing their abilities
- Think about what they can learn
- Engage with the mistake with a desire to correct it
- Embrace novelty to master new skills
- Look for people who challenge them to grow
- Take responsibility for their failures
- Focus on the process and learning without obsessing about the outcome
- Find inspiration in others' success
- Accept criticism as a way to learn

PEOPLE WITH A GROWTH MINDSET

Learn from mistakes	Persevere through failures
Take responsibility	Look for growth
Find inspiration in others success	Embrace challenges
Accept criticism	Believe skills can be built

LEADING WITH A FALSE GROWTH MINDSET

Wondering if you have a fixed or a growth mindset? We will get to it in the next section in this chapter. But for now, be aware that it's easy to develop misconceptions about the growth mindset. It's actually worse to believe that you have a growth mindset when your behavior and actions clearly state otherwise. If you have a fixed mindset and you are aware of it, you can at least make an attempt to develop a growth mindset. However, if you have a false growth mindset[9], you can drift away from indulging in practices that build abilities and fosters growth.

You are leading with a wrong version of the growth mindset if:

1. You believe growth mindset is binary
2. You fail to connect effort with progress
3. You discount the importance of other factors in your success
4. You keep pushing in the wrong direction

#1: You believe growth mindset is binary

It isn't hard to imagine people who proclaim to have a growth mindset even when their actions are rooted in a fixed mindset. Either they don't want to accept their fixed mindset or lack a proper understanding of the growth mindset.

This large disconnect is often due to the mistaken belief that a growth mindset is binary - you either have it or you don't. Growth mindset is not an attribute that defines you, it's one component of your thinking. Much like multiple beliefs that co-exist in your mind, both fixed and growth mindset sit close together and show up in different areas of your life. They get triggered in different situations. You can very well have a growth mindset when it comes to solving complex problems but may fall back on a fixed mindset in social situations. You may exhibit a growth mindset when it comes to encouraging your child to practice their piano lessons while feeling limited in your own abilities to learn a new language.

Consider this. Your boss assigns you a problem at work that you have never solved before. Since you don't know how to solve the problem yet, you put together a plan to solve it. You read all the relevant material on the topic, put that learning into practice by developing a prototype, seek feedback from colleagues to improve upon your work, and ask for help when you feel stuck. That's your growth mindset guiding you to embrace the challenge and apply different strategies to complete your project. In another instance, while learning to play tennis, you may find yourself putting in the effort, but do not notice a significant improvement in your strokes. Instead of looking inward to your process, you may decide to quit with the conclusion "Others can do it because they are talented. I don't have what it takes to learn tennis."

Instead of a proclamation "I am a growth-minded person," learn to identify different situations in which invoking a growth mindset can make a difference. Think about what will help you move forward instead of holding you back due to fear of failure, lack of abilities, or anxiety of the unknown.

#2: You fail to connect effort with progress

Effort does matter. Without effort, you may have all the talent in the world and still accomplish nothing. However, simply putting in the effort won't take you very far. If you keep failing and do not try new strategies, will you get the results that you want? When you are trying to build new skills, will practicing what you already know and feel easier help you improve? When struggling with something, if you refuse to reach out and gain knowledge and support from your network, will you make the right kind of progress? When you make mistakes, if you simply continue what you were doing earlier and do not take time to learn from your mistakes, will you succeed?

Research points out "It's not just about effort. You also need to learn skills that let you use your brain in a smarter way. ... You actually have to practice the right way ... to get better at something. In fact, scientists have found that the brain grows more when you learn something new, and less when you practice things you already know."[10] It means working harder to think deeply about problems, reflecting on how to solve them through different strategies, making adjustments to different approaches, and solutioning based on feedback collected along the way. It means not sticking to one way of doing things and rather exploring creative ways to pursue new ideas.

Consider this. You decide to run a marathon and start with a daily morning practice routine. Soon, you notice that you can't seem to go beyond 10 miles without breaking down. You start out strong, but end up tired, fatigued, and frustrated. You keep putting in the effort by doing the same workouts every week but fail to make progress on your goals. In this case, simply putting in the effort by sticking to your current strategy won't help you move forward. Perhaps you need different training sessions or more strength training, or a different pacing approach or fuelling plan. By re-evaluating your effort and developing a strategic plan of runs that vary in distance and effort, your chances of reaching your goals will be much, much higher.

To get better at something, you need to practice the right way as the kind of effort - effort that stretches your brain and teaches you something new - counts more than the amount of effort.

#3: You discount the importance of other factors in your success

Barbara Oakley, professor of Engineering whose online courses on learning are some of the most popular MOOC classes in the world rightly said "People can often do more, change more, and learn more—often far more—than they've ever dreamed possible. Our potential is hidden in plain sight all around us."[11] She is absolutely right. Isn't this what a growth mindset is all about?

I am all up for the belief that we can grow our abilities if we put effort, apply the right strategies and seek help from others. However, thinking that "we can be anything we want to be only if we put our mind to it" discounts the importance of other factors beyond our mindset in our success. It seems to focus on the fact that the only determinant of success is our mindset.[12] We all know that's not the case. Context, culture, and the environment around us matter too. Our luck plays a crucial role in whether we succeed in our goals or not. We are also not all created equal - some people have better resources and opportunities and are equipped to take more risks and invest more time and money into achieving success.

Let's understand some of these factors:

Opportunities: Not everyone has equal access and opportunity to the road to success. Where we are born, how we are raised, our education, wealth, and many other factors play a role in the kind of opportunities we get and seek in life. Bill Gates got access to expensive computers and the opportunity to learn programming as an eight grader in 1968. While there's no doubt that he's brilliant, it's the extraordinary series of opportunities that put him apart from many others and helped him achieve success.

Culture: Our culture influences what we think about ourselves and how we behave with others. In many cultures, women are expected to be responsible for things that men are not. They are expected to look and behave in certain ways. These strong cultural dynamics impact the success of many young women. Women still continue to fight stereotyping and gender bias to succeed in the workplace. As a female, you may keep getting passed up for a leadership role even though you may be the most promising candidate in your organization. It isn't your mindset holding you back. You need to fight the culture that discriminates against women at work.

Luck: We tend to mistake success for competence. While qualities like perseverance, intellectual curiosity, and openness to embrace challenges are essential to success, there's a lot of variance that's often left unexplained. Research shows that our luck plays a far greater role in our success than we realize.[13] While luck is not everything, placing an exclusive focus on our qualities can make us overlook randomness that plays out in subtler ways, causing us to ignore explanations that involve luck.

With less resources at hand, life struggles can sometimes get in the way. This does not mean that you should stop trying with the belief that you will never succeed anyway. That will be adopting a fixed mindset. Rather, use your growth mindset to improve the process, care about learning and enjoy the journey instead of a single-minded focus on the destination you need to reach.

#4: You keep pushing in the wrong direction

Becoming delusional and pushing hard in the wrong direction without looking back to examine your decisions may throw you right off the bat even before you have started. As Stephen R. Covey points out in his book *The 7 Habits of Highly Effective People,* "How different our lives are when we really know what is deeply important to us, and, keeping that picture in mind, we manage ourselves each day to be and to do what really matters most. If the ladder is not leaning against the right wall, every step we take just gets us to the wrong place faster."[14]

A growth mindset isn't intended to get in the way of effective living. In no way it implies taking on more and more responsibilities with the belief that you can do it all. Yes, building new skills and learning anything new requires stretching yourself, but it isn't an excuse to work extra hard and compromise on your health. Stress and exhaustion from overwork can kill the joy of the learning process. You can grow without killing yourself in the process by staying realistic with your goals and targeting incremental improvements instead of one major leap in your abilities.

Remember, a growth mindset is about implementing the right strategies to advance in your goals. This requires making the best use of available resources, saying no to work that does not align with your goals, and putting effort into activities that matter. We will learn more about this in later sections in the book.

WHAT'S YOUR MINDSET?

To bring about any change, a good place to start is to know where you stand right now. What's your mindset? Unless you make an attempt to identify what your fixed mindset triggers are, you cannot apply strategies and retrain your brain to be more growth-oriented.

Keep in mind that no one has only one mindset. Our thinking in different circumstances triggers different emotional reactions and can either take us down a fixed mindset path where we stop believing in growing our abilities or a growth mindset path where we strive hard to maintain motivation and believe in achieving success through hard work, effort, and experience.

Throughout the book, I will give you exercises to help you think deeply about the topic and apply new strategies to put your learning into practice. Remember, to learn and not to do is really not to learn. You can revisit any of these exercises later or repeat them for mastering new skills. All the resources in this book are available online. You can either do these exercises in a notebook or take a printout of the templates available online. Download all the resources once and put them to practice as you proceed with the various exercises in this book.

Complete the following exercise to determine your predominant mindset. Take a moment to read each of the scenarios below and choose the description from columns B and C that best describes your behavior or how you typically think about different things in your life.

Try to be completely honest. Remember, there are no right or wrong answers. What matters is that you stay true to yourself when you attempt this exercise.

Exercise: What's your mindset?

SCENARIO	I TEND TO THINK (B)	I TEND TO THINK (C)
A negotiation that didn't go well	Good negotiators are born and it can't be changed very much	Negotiation qualities can be built with practice and experience
When taking on a new challenge	I don't have what it takes and everyone will find out if I fail	This is a great opportunity for me to improve and enhance my skills
You struggle with a project	My abilities limit me to achieve the outcomes I want. There is no point in	What can I do better / How can I take this forward

	trying if I am going to fail	
You receive criticism	This feedback measures my capabilities / People are being too judgmental / It's a personal attack	I can separate words from intent and find some value in this feedback
Your co-worker gets promoted and you didn't	I will never be as good as they are / I feel jealous of their smartness / My boss is clearly biased	I can be successful too if I try harder / What can I learn from their success
You fail in your attempt to reach a goal	This is my limit. I can't learn anymore / I can't get any better even if I try	What does this failure teach me / How can I do better next time
When you disagree with someone	I am concerned that my ideas will be rejected or others will find me dumb. So, I choose to keep quiet	I share my honest opinion and openly express my disagreement
Procrastinating on a task	I am lazy and incapable of achieving my goals / I can't do it /	My determination and effort are the measures of my

	There's no point in trying	outcomes. I must try
When evaluating a risk	Don't take it. Failure will affect your reputation	What data do I need to make a decision / How can I learn from others / What does my past teach me
When seeking clarification on tasks or goals	I will look weak and incompetent for asking these questions	Better clarity will help me move forward in the right direction / I will learn something new by asking these questions
Working against an aggressive deadline	I will never meet this deadline. It's better to give up now	What strategies and practices can I employ to meet this deadline / Who can help
You made a mistake	I am so stupid / Others will think I am not smart / I am a complete failure / I am hopeless / I am not responsible for this mistake	What went wrong / How can I fix it / What do I learn from it / How can I do better next time

When collaborating with others	I say and do things that makes me look smart / I look for approval and validation	I try to learn from others / I openly express my opinion / I do what's right, not what's popular
When meeting someone new	I brag about my accomplishments / I try to look good by saying intelligent things / I am worried about how they will judge me	I look for things I can learn from them / I try to ask questions
While giving feedback to others	I say only nice things about them even if I don't mean them / I do not say anything that might hurt their feelings even if it's the right thing to do / I try to stay in their good books	I state my intent and give them feedback that will help them grow even if it makes them feel sad in the short-term
In a meeting	I use my power to influence and control others / I speak up only to establish my competence / I care less about the	I speak up to seek clarification, ask questions or state my opinion. My intent is to enable the group to put all the information out

guides you to build your abilities, learn and grow through effort, practice and persistence.
- Growth mindset is not a state you can achieve. It's a component of your thinking. Your fixed mindset and growth mindset triggers in different situations. Important thing is to realize when invoking a growth mindset can make a difference.
- To get better at something, effort counts, but it's the right kind of effort that matters more. Effort that involves new strategies, learning from your mistakes, and that stretches your brain and teaches you something new.
- The key to unlock your future potential is in developing a growth mindset and it starts with self-awareness of where you stand right now.
- Practicing a growth mindset requires committing to a lifelong journey. There are no shortcuts.

growth mindset. By embracing your current mindset, you will feel empowered to challenge it and grow it further.

If you already show signs of a growth mindset, don't stop now. Take it to the next level. Read through the remaining chapters to strengthen your growth mindset by learning new strategies and putting them into practice. Remember, a growth mindset is not a state you accomplish. You need to be self-aware to identify the opportunities where applying a growth mindset will make a difference and continually invest in learning better practices to champion this mindset.

Mindset is not like height or the color of your eyes that's part of your genetic code and you can't do much to change it. It's more like a language that you can learn at any age. It's never too late to develop a growth mindset. People often say - *Growth mindset is for kids! I am too old! I can't possibly develop a growth mindset now!* These limiting beliefs are also part of your fixed mindset. The next chapter will help you understand why the growth mindset is for everyone, regardless of age and how you can use your brain to do wonderful things once you learn how it works.

Chapter Summary

- Mindsets are powerful beliefs that determine how you experience the events in your life and what actions you take. Your beliefs are a creation of your mind and you can change them.
- You can either choose a fixed mindset that limits you by believing that talent, intelligence, and potential is fixed and no amount of effort can change it or a growth mindset that

| In a career you don't like | These are the only skills I have / I am good at my job and others always appreciate me. It doesn't matter if I don't like it / I don't have the talent to try something new | What do I want / How can I build the skills to try something new / Who can help me in growing my abilities |

You can download a printable version of "What's Your Mindset" at: techtello.com/upgrade-your-mindset/templates/

While going through each of the scenarios above, assign a score of 1 to each response you select from columns B (2nd) and C (3rd). Now sum up your total score for both the columns.

Fixed mindset score = Sum of score from column B

Growth mindset score = Sum of score from column C

My fixed mindset score is _____

My growth mindset score is _____

My predominant mindset is _____

Your score shows a predominant fixed mindset? The remaining chapters in this book will help you take incremental steps towards a

	decision and more about proving my worth	in the open so that we can make a better decision
When you achieve success	I try to take all the credit / I celebrate my success and bask in its glory. There's nothing more to be done	I share credit with people who helped me succeed / I celebrate my success and then think about "what's next"
In a social situation	I do not approach others with the fear that they will judge me / I try to say smart things / I am constantly worried about what others might think about me	I may feel uncomfortable, but I try to make a conversation / I listen intently to other people's opinions / I look for opportunities to learn
When others blame you	I get defensive and try to save my reputation / I justify my innocence without hearing them out / I know they are wrong	I ask questions to clarify how they have come to this conclusion / I may not agree with them, but I do not try to enforce my viewpoint. Rather I look to learn from the situation

CHAPTER 2

Start With Brain

GROWING UP if you have been constantly criticized for your mistakes and told that you are not good enough, you can't succeed and you have no talent, these limiting beliefs can become an unconscious truth for your brain. Now, you cannot possibly blame yourself for your environment and the people in it whose notions guided a large part of your life. But you can take things under your control and not let someone else's opinion become your reality.

It's never too late to change your beliefs that can empower you instead of holding you back. That's because your brain can be rewired. It can learn new tricks. You can do things that seemed impossible or too hard to do earlier. Your brain has the amazing ability to change, adapt, and get stronger, not only as a kid but also as you get older.[1]

Learning to ride a bike, teaching yourself to swim, reading a book, or even walking as a baby were skills you once didn't have. How did you build these skills - by observing, listening, and practicing. You may not realize it, but the structure of your brain changes every time you learn something new. You have a physical limit, but your brain is infinitely malleable. Training your brain in the direction of your goals can lift you towards your potential.

Research has shown that your brain cells aren't fixed and they change their structure in response to new experiences.[2] Everything you do affects it - tackling challenging puzzles, watching TV, playing video games, creating art, learning a new language. What does this mean? The more you challenge your mind, the more it will grow. Just like exercising your body helps you build muscles, exercising your brain keeps it strong and working at its best. Think of it this way - your brain is a series of circuits and pathways and every time you experience something and decide to act on it, it fires a pathway. When you do something consistently, the same pathway fires multiple times and strengthens the circuit. With enough practice, what was once difficult becomes second nature.

- Want to learn to reason well? Exercise your brain and practice reasoning skills. Pick activities that require a logical connection between ideas. Participate in debates, solve sudoku, crossword puzzles, and brain teasers.
- Public speaking makes you uncomfortable? Get yourself some gigs and practice in front of real people.
- Dancing is your thing? Spend time learning different dance techniques. Find your style, build flexibility, and practice routines.

- Want to learn a new language? Find a friend or colleague who speaks the language. Visualize, vocalize, use gestures, and practice the language in real life.
- Trying to get better at Chess? Play lots and lots of games, review your moves, study others, experiment and practice through puzzles and online competitions.

You can grow your intelligence.[3] You can also have a stronger, smarter brain only if you can get past your beliefs that make you want to give up. Dr. Michael Merzenich, a neuroscientist at the University of California, San Francisco and pioneer in brain plasticity research did experiments that showed that the brain was massively plastic at an older age. He says "That's what makes it so fabulous. Everyone has the capacity to be better at virtually everything. With that understanding, miracles can occur in your capacity to understand or do complicated things that you never thought you would be able to do. You are designed to be continuously improvable. Nobody has defined what their limits are. I can tell you whatever you think your limits are, you are wrong. You can be better next week, a little bit. But in a year you can be a lot better in almost anything that matters to you."[4]

You aren't stuck with what you have and practice can help you reorganize your brain to master new skills. Let's dive into how you can achieve this.

FIRST: STEP INTO THE ARENA

If you want to know how to do anything, you can get most of the information at the touch of a button. It's all out there. You can read books, listen to podcasts, attend workshops, watch videos, or take online courses. All this information can leave you inspired, energized, impressed, and at times even mesmerized. And yet none of it will have a lasting impact on your life. All the knowledge in the world cannot turn your desires into the outcomes you wish to achieve. Because you don't lack information. What you lack is putting that information into action.

Imagine this. You are learning to give a presentation and spend hours watching videos, reading books, articles, asking questions, and learning strategies from people around you. However, you do not put your knowledge to practice. Will your skills improve? Indulging in mental practice by rehearsing the presentation in your mind, visualizing that you are delivering it, imagining everything in vivid detail, hearing the sounds you would hear, feeling the feelings you would feel can be a useful technique to get better, but it's only by giving the actual presentation that you can get significantly better. Knowledge can help you in triggering the right behavior but the only way to grow is to sustain action.

Here's another one. In your attempt to move from an individual contributor to a management role, you pour yourself into management books, read every material you can get your hands on, and keenly observe other senior people in your organization to see it in practice. But whenever an opportunity comes along, you do not apply what you have learnt. Will you have the skills to be a great manager someday? What looks good in theory, sometimes does not work out in real life. You need to put yourself out there, experience the real thing, and then only you can incrementally build the skills required to be a great manager someday. Practice involves making mistakes and mistakes are essential to learning. You can't exercise your brain muscles by watching from the sidelines, you actually need to step into the arena and be part of the game.

Growth mindset = Belief that you can grow

How can you grow = By putting your beliefs into action

Just like sand on a beach, your brain bears the footprints of the decisions you have made, the skills you have learnt, and the actions you have taken.[5] To be good at anything, you have to turn these footprints into pathways. You have to fire the same circuits, not once or twice, but multiple times to allow your brain to strengthen these signals, and to make things easier that were once difficult.

When you were first learning to swim, cycle or run, remember being told that in order to get stronger, your muscles need to struggle? This applies to your brain too. If you keep doing what comes easy and push difficult stuff to the side, you won't learn and grow. Research suggests that adding specific types of challenges to learning in the form of creating desirable difficulties can help you become a better learner.[6]

Effort matters, but it's the right kind of effort that matters more - one that stretches your brain. So, if you are putting effort and not seeing progress, ask yourself "are you putting effort that stretches and expands your skills or simply tracking the quantity of effort without checking for its quality?"

Think of it this way - you and your friend are learning to code. You keep writing similar pieces of code, ones that come easy to you and make you feel good. While your friend keeps pushing to the next level. Even though she struggles through them, she persists and works harder to solve difficult problems. Who do you think will be a better programmer after one year?

Let's take another example. Assume that there are many opportunities for growth in your workplace. You keep opting for safe bets, ones you have mastered and acquired a know-how. Another colleague in your workplace opts for the challenges that push her to build new skills, requires her to devise better strategies for success, and try harder to tackle the unknowns involved in the process. Who do you think will have the skills and the experience required to handle higher-level responsibilities at work?

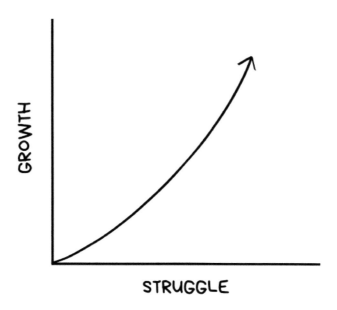

Less Struggle = Less Growth

More Struggle = More Growth

This passage referred to as "*The Man in the Arena*" from the speech given by Theodore Roosevelt describes how struggle is essential to effort "It is not the critic who counts; not the man who points out how the strong man stumbles, or where the doer of deeds could have done them better. The credit belongs to the man who is actually in the arena, whose face is marred by dust and sweat and blood; who strives valiantly; who errs, who comes short again and again, because there is no effort without error and shortcoming; but who does actually strive to do the deeds; who knows great enthusiasms, the great devotions; who spends himself in a worthy cause; who at the best knows in the end the triumph of high achievement, and who at the worst, if he fails, at least fails while daring greatly, so that his place shall never be with those cold and timid souls who neither know victory nor defeat."[7]

Growth mindset = Belief that you can grow

How can you grow = Consistent Action + More struggle

The rest of the chapter is dedicated to putting your growth mindset into action. We will start off with an understanding of the power of language in triggering the right behavior, learn about the importance of aligning your actions to your identity, and then work on other strategies to stay on course when the going gets tough.

SECOND: CHANGE THE WAY YOU TALK TO YOURSELF

Angela Duckworth, an academic, psychologist, and author of *Grit* tells a story about a spring semester in her first year of college at Harvard when she enrolled in neurobiology. Once while taking a test, as the test got harder, she began to panic and started thinking: *I'm not going to finish! I have no idea what I'm doing! I'm going to fail!*[8] The more she thought about them, the less she could focus on the questions. When she got a bad grade the first time and then again during midterm, she knew she had a choice to make. She can either engage in self-defeating thoughts: *I'm an idiot! Nothing I do is good enough!* and drop out of the class or she can be hopeful: *I won't quit! I can figure this out!*

She tried harder, practiced the most difficult problems, and attained a level of mastery where nothing could surprise her. She didn't give up and aced her finals. While her negative self-talk could have made her drop out of class, it was the positive self-talk that helped her in directing her energy towards achieving her goals.

Fixed Mindset Language

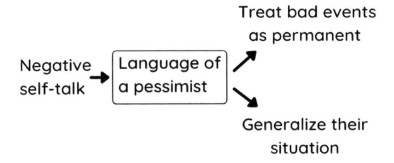

Growth Mindset Language

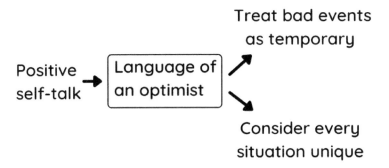

Author and psychologist Martin Seligman, who studied the *I won't quit* response to adversity in people describes two categories of people.[9] Some people as he calls them "pessimists" attach permanent and pervasive explanations to bad events - permanence signifying that you can't do much about them and pervasive in that one single event can influence a large part of your life. Permanent and pervasive explanations turn minor events into major setbacks and these people gravitate towards *"I quit attitude."*

On the other end of the spectrum are "optimists," those who use temporary and specific explanations to describe bad events - temporary explanations motivate them to put effort into fixing their problems and specificity keeps the focus of the problem on that particular event without generalizing it. Temporary and specific explanations drive clarity and encourage problem-solving. Such people learn to take control of their situation and don't feel helpless.

Words have power. Shifting from negative self-talk in the form of permanent and pervasive interpretations to positive self-talk using temporary and specific explanations can enable you to act on your situation and do something about it. Let's say you missed a deadline to deliver a project. Instead of saying *"I'm a loser! I screw everything up!"* choose to say *"I did not manage my time well. I could have been less distracted. I can procrastinate less and start earlier."*

Think about the recent events in your life - fight with a coworker, a lost deal, a missed sales target, being passed up for promotion, receiving criticism for your work, losing a client, or any other scenario. What language did you use to describe these events? The way you talk to yourself plays a key role in how you lead your life. As Ryan Holiday says in his book, *The Obstacle Is the Way* "You will come across obstacles in life -- fair and unfair. And you will discover, time and time again, that what matters most is not what these obstacles are but how we see them, how we react to them, and whether we keep our composure. You will learn that this reaction determines how successful we will be in overcoming -- or possibly thriving because of -- them. Where one person sees a crisis, another can see opportunity. Where one is blinded by success, another sees reality with ruthless objectivity. Where one loses control of emotions, another can remain calm."[10]

With practice, you can modify your self-talk. Take a note of your emotions and whenever you sense going down a negative path, reframe it using a more positive tone. Use language that describes the event as temporary and specific, hence fixable as opposed to a permanent and pervasive explanation with a feeling of hopelessness. When you make mistakes, instead of saying *"I can't do anything right"* choose to say *"I made a mistake. I can fix it."* When you struggle through a task, instead of saying *"I don't have what it takes,"* choose to say *"I can figure this out."*

Saying is believing. If you keep telling yourself that you can't do something, ultimately your brain will believe it. Don't let your negative self-talk become a self-fulfilling prophecy. To develop a growth mindset, learn to use the right language.

Joanna Zeiger, former Olympic triathlete, says the consistent practice of repeating strong words or sentences can go a long way. "Write it down so that you can go back to it," she says. "Then whenever you hit a rough patch, pull those words out so that you can overcome any negativity you're experiencing."[11]

Take a printout of the grid below and stick it where you can see it or keep a digital version on your phone so that you can use it whenever you need it. Now, whenever you find yourself engaging in negative self-talk (1st column below), shift to positive framing by using language from the 2nd column. To make it more effective, write it down.

Exercise: Change the way you talk to yourself

WHAT DID YOU TELL YOURSELF	WHAT CAN YOU TELL YOURSELF
I am either good or I am not	I can get better with practice
I can't do it	I can do it. What do I need to learn to make it work?
I don't get it	It seems hard, but I will not give up
My work is not good enough	I can improve my work
I do not have the ability to learn	I am capable of learning
It's better to stick to what I know	I want to explore new strategies
I can't deal with this	Whatever happens, I will handle it
I have fixed potential	I have more potential
This is frustrating	It's ok to fail. I probably need a new strategy.
I am who I am	I can be who I wish to be
This is hard	I just don't know how to do this yet

Others can do it, but I can't	I can do it too. What am I missing?
What I know is good enough	There's always more to learn
This is not my strength	I will turn it into my strength
I am not smart	I can learn and grow
I mess up all the time. I am so stupid.	I could have handled it better. What can I learn from my mistakes?
I don't deserve anything	I can achieve what my heart desires
I can't seem to get anything right	I can fix things
I don't have what it takes	I can figure it out. There must be a way around this.
I am not going to get any better at this	I will give it another try
I have no idea what I am doing	I won't quit and work it all out
There's no way it will work	I will do everything possible to make it work
I have never done this before	It's an opportunity to learn something new
I don't have the resources	Who can help me?

| I am a failure | Everyone makes mistakes. What can I do now? |

You can download a printable version of "Change the Way You Talk to Yourself" at:
techtello.com/upgrade-your-mindset/templates/

Changing language without taking action won't get you the results. Words have little meaning unless you also act on them. Later in this book, we will learn strategies and tactics on how to put your beliefs to action so that you can experience the benefits of believing in your abilities and feel inspired to try harder.

THIRD: SHAPE YOUR IDENTITY

If all throughout life, in school, college, and at home, you have been given labels - smart, not smart, shy, outspoken, introvert, extrovert, athletic, not creative, or not a math person, then over time you start believing in these labels. They become an essential part of your being, the fabric of who you are. Your identity shapes up based on the beliefs you hold and these labels drive your thinking. You take certain actions thinking "this is who I am" and resist others with the notion "this is not me."

- I am terrible at cooking.
- I am not a sports person.
- I am too reckless to drive.
- I am horrible with puzzles.

- I am not good with numbers.

Anything you try to do which is not in alignment with your identity won't last long. The conflict with the self will be too strong to implement any everlasting change. You can convince yourself to practice a growth mindset and may even succeed once or twice, but if you don't shape your identity, it will be hard to stick to it in the long term. To make changes long-term, you have to make them part of your identity so that anything you do is a reflection of your identity and does not conflict with it.

BELIEFS BECOME IDENTITY

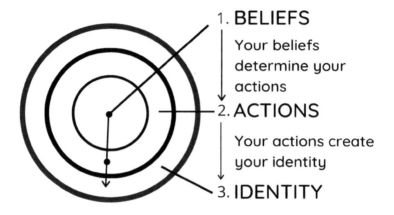

1. **BELIEFS**
   Your beliefs determine your actions
2. **ACTIONS**
   Your actions create your identity
3. **IDENTITY**

IDENTITY SHAPES BELIEFS

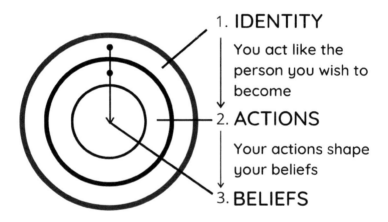

1. **IDENTITY**
   You act like the person you wish to become
2. **ACTIONS**
   Your actions shape your beliefs
3. **BELIEFS**

James Clear, author of *Atomic Habits* says, "Most people don't even consider identity change when they set out to improve. They set goals and determine the actions they should take to achieve those goals without considering the beliefs that drive their actions. They never shift the way they look at themselves, and they don't realize that their old identity can sabotage their new plans for change."[12]

James Clear describes three layers of change:[13]

The first layer is changing your outcomes. This level is concerned with changing your results: losing weight, publishing a book, winning a championship. Most of the goals you set are associated with this level of change.

The second layer is changing your process. This level is concerned with changing your habits and systems: implementing a new routine at the gym, decluttering your desk for better workflow, developing a meditation practice. Most of the habits you build are associated with this level.

The third and deepest layer is changing your identity. This level is concerned with changing your beliefs: your worldview, your self-image, your judgments about yourself and others. Most of the beliefs, assumptions, and biases you hold are associated with this level.

True change in mindset can happen only through an identity change. Your identity should be more than a mere title or the outcomes you wish to achieve. It should be about the behaviors and actions of the person you wish to become. Once you have defined the person you wish to become, you can align your actions with it.

When you start with limiting beliefs, you let those beliefs guide your actions. Your actions then create your identity. However, when you start with identity, you can choose to act like the person you wish to become. Your actions shape your beliefs which further strengthens your identity.

Starting with limiting beliefs:

- You believe that you can never be good at public speaking. With this belief, you are more self-conscious when speaking publicly, which makes you falter more. This further reinforces your identity "I am not a good speaker."
- You believe that you can never lose weight. With this belief, you do not even try. You do not include healthy practices in your routine which reinforces your identity "I am not healthy."

Starting with identity:

- You want to build the identity of a person who's good at public speaking. Your identity gives you the motivation to practice public speaking skills. With practice and consistency, you get better and that shapes your belief "I can be good at public speaking."
- You want to build the identity of a healthy person. Your identity gives you the motivation to make changes to your life and include healthy practices like exercising and eating healthy food. Every small improvement shapes your belief "I can be a healthy person."

If you want to build the identity of a growth mindset person, you have to think about the behaviors and actions of a growth mindset person. You have to let go of the labels that impact your confidence and personal growth, unlearn past beliefs and challenge your thinking. Instead of fitting inside a mould, you have to learn to find freedom in exploring interests, setting new goals, and expecting better outcomes.

- To run a successful startup, think about the useful behaviors and actions of a leader - future orientation, perseverance despite failures, who champions learning. What's not helpful - avoiding conflicts, my way or the highway attitude, lacking influence.
- To become a writer, think about the useful behaviors and actions of a writer - write consistently, publish content, embrace imperfection, open to changes. What's not helpful - plagiarizing somebody else's hard work, making excuses to miss deadlines, responding to negative reviews with negativity.
- To become a chef, think about the useful behaviors and actions of a chef - creativity, attention to detail, willingness to accept criticism, handle high-stress environments. What's not helpful - lack of trust for staff, short fuse, aggressive body language.

Complete the following exercise to shape your identity. Do this exercise for the different roles you play in your life - as a parent, spouse, community helper, friend, worker, etc. Remember, you can have a growth mindset in one aspect of your life and a fixed mindset in another. So, doing this exercise for every important relationship in your life will help you develop a growth mindset in each.

It may be hard the first time you attempt to put it in writing. But if you start taking a conscious look at your life and think about who you wish to become in each role, certain ideas will start to emerge. Keep coming back to this exercise and take notes of your thought process. Write down everything you think derails you from building this identity and everything that reinforces it.

Exercise: Shape your identity

For every role in your life,

As a _____

1. Who do you wish to become?

   _____

   _____

2. Describe the essential qualities of that person

   _____

   _____

3. What behaviors can prevent you from building this identity?

   _____

   _____

4. What behaviors can be useful in reinforcing this identity?

   _____

   _____

You can download a printable version of "Shape Your Identity" at: techtello.com/upgrade-your-mindset/templates/

Each time you find yourself with a fixed mindset, remind yourself of this identity and ask if the person you wish to become will think like this:

- Instead of thinking about whether you can do something or not, think about whether you want to be the person who gives up easily.
- Instead of thinking about whether you can succeed or not, think about how a person who wants to succeed will act.
- Instead of feeling limited by your abilities, think about what a person who wants to build new skills will do.

FOURTH: IMITATE THE PEOPLE YOU ADMIRE

Our subconscious mind works in strange ways. As Daniel Kahneman, psychologist and economist notable for his work on the psychology of judgment and decision-making puts it "Most impressions and thoughts arise in your conscious experience without your knowing how they got there. You cannot trace how you came to the belief that there is a lamp on the desk in front of you, or how you detected a hint of irritation in your spouse's voice on the telephone, or how you managed to avoid a threat on the road before you became consciously aware of it. The mental work that produces impressions, intuitions, and many decisions goes on in silence in our mind."[14]

Often people drive back home from work in the evening with no memory of how they got there. While your conscious mind was hard at work planning other important events in your life, it was your unconscious mind that got you home safely. You may wonder - how was your unconscious mind aware of your goal to reach home and how did it make all the decisions typically required to navigate traffic on the way, like stopping at traffic lights and the route to take?

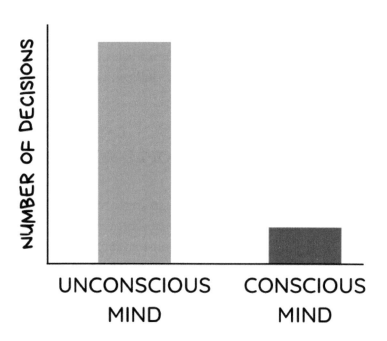

Your unconscious mind picks up the cues in your environment like the setting sun, sitting in your car, and turning on the engine as a sign it's time to head home. Also, when the same goal is triggered multiple times, your mind learns to do it effortlessly. The more you repeat something, the more automatic it gets. Next time the pattern repeats, you no longer need to engage actively with it, your unconscious makes the decisions behind the scenes for you.[15]

Look at it this way. Your unconscious mind is really a gift. With the limited processing power of your conscious mind, you won't be able to achieve much in life. It's your unconscious mind that comes to the rescue with its ability to handle large amounts of information and make quick decisions for you. The side-effect - a large part of the decisions you make every day operate without your awareness. Yes, you may not even realize how you react to failures, what you do when faced with tough situations or why you give up easily without trying when dealing with something hard. Your unconscious has learnt from your past reactions and makes these decisions for you.

What if you feed your unconscious mind with the behaviors expected of a growth mindset person? Let's see how you can do that so that your unconscious mind operates with the same goals as the ones you want to choose voluntarily. But first a question for you - are you surrounded by people who practice a growth mindset, those who do not collapse in the face of failures and bounce back after a temporary rough patch or you spend a large part of your time with fixed mindset people who spiral into hopelessness after encountering even one bout of failure? Think about this for a moment before reading ahead.

Motivational speaker Jim Rohn famously said, "We are the average of the five people we spend the most time with." Your unconscious mind is at play often observing and silently absorbing the behavior of those around you. You may not realize it, but people close to you influence your thinking in huge ways. Ever noticed how your tone changes when you are around a certain group of people - you copy the way they talk, tune into their behaviors and even act like them. These imitations become prominent when you are close to someone or admire them as you tend to pay more attention to them. Without your conscious awareness, your mind adopts the behaviors and practices of those around you.[16] Now, you may realize why being around fixed mindset people isn't such a good idea.

You can leverage the power of imitation to develop a growth mindset by following this three-step process:

1. Surround yourself with growth mindset people.
2. Let the group guide you towards the right behavior.
3. Reinforce your personal identity by being part of the shared identity.

Surround yourself with growth mindset people

Look around and find people you admire who also practice a growth mindset. It could be your boss who's always pushing you for improvement, your spouse who never fails to amaze you with their determination, a friend who's known to push boundaries, a mentor who inspires you to grow, or even your child who seems to never give up and takes joy in learning. Literally anyone you have access to can be a powerful source for feeding your mind with the right cues. Let's call them your "growth buddies."

Let the group guide you towards the right behavior

Spend more and more time around your growth buddies, observe them, talk to them and discuss the strategies you can put into practice. While you are consciously discussing ideas to build a growth mindset, your unconscious mind will do its job behind the scenes to strengthen these beliefs.

Being surrounded by people who have the skills you admire not only helps you in putting them into practice, they also serve as an inspiration during difficult moments. While overcoming challenges when you are unsure of how to act or when you find yourself spiraling into a fixed mindset, draw inspiration from these people and ask yourself "what will they do in this scenario?"

Reinforce your personal identity by being part of the shared identity

In the previous section *"Shape Your Identity,"* we discussed the importance of aligning your behavior and actions with your identity. Being surrounded by people who demonstrate the behavior you are trying to build will strengthen your identity, always serving as a reminder about the actions you need to take to build this identity. Once you link your identity to this group, you are no longer pursuing individual goals. You are on a shared journey that motivates you to adopt practices with long-lasting effects.

Be careful of the downside though. It works the other way round too if you are surrounded by bad influences. Who you hang out with is who you become. Choose carefully.

FINALLY: MIX IT TO FIX IT

Every day in life we run into brand new problems that do not come with a manual, where our standard procedures do not work, and even solutions from our past experience in similar situations don't work out. A great marketing campaign that fails for no obvious reasons. A deal that falls through despite showing strong signs of success. An otherwise happy toddler gets cranky and refuses to calm down. A client who turns their back on you overnight. Your friends and family refuse to support you when you need money. You miss the audition you have waited for a long time.

What do you do in such situations? You get down to work actively chasing a new connection in your brain to solve your problem. You try harder and harder to focus on your problem, exerting a lot of mental energy in the process, but find yourself stuck at an impasse - a connection in your brain you want to make but can't. You desperately need the insight to make progress. It's exactly at these moments that you can slip into fixed ways of thinking - *I can't do this! I don't have what it takes! I am terrible at it! I will never get this right!* Eventually, if nothing seems to work, it must be an issue with your talent. You simply don't have what it takes.

David Rock, author of *Your Brain At Work* says, "When you get stuck, do something totally different even for a few seconds and then come back to the problem. Sometimes your conscious processing capacity is itself the problem. Get it out of the way, and the solution appears."[17] What does this mean? It's not your incorrect strategy or lack of talent that gets in the way of solving a problem, it's your own brain looking for a few spare moments to build the right connections. Disconnect from the problem for even a few seconds, do something different and then get back to it - play your favorite music, do exercise, go for a walk, take a nap, make yourself a cup of coffee, or do something creative. Anything that takes your mind off the problem might help you see it more clearly and you will have a better chance of solving it later.

At the beginning of this chapter, I mentioned that our brain is like a muscle that grows with practice. What I did not mention was it also gets tired after a long session of deep focussed work and once depleted, it's less effective.[18] What makes it even more interesting is how energy spent in one part of our brain only causes fatigue in that part of the brain while the rest of the brain muscles are free to be exercised. When you spend a large amount of time planning at work, your brain may get exhausted from all the thinking, problem-solving, and focussing that's typically required in a planning exercise, but you may be surprised to know that you still have a lot of energy left to do other things, like attending meetings, reading, responding to emails, or chatting with a coworker. That's because the part of the brain that does deep thinking during problem-solving is different from the one that does mundane things like chatting.

Ever wondered why school days aren't structured to have one subject the entire day and rather divided into 45-60 mins blocks of time for each subject? It's because doing Science for a full day on Monday, English on Tuesday, and Maths on Wednesday would be a highly ineffective way to learn. Instead of practicing Maths several hours in a row, a better strategy is to mix it up with English, Science, and other subjects alternating between them to let your brain recover.

Thinking	Routine	Break	Meeting
B1	B2	B3	B4
Planning, Problem Solving	Emails, Chats	Coffee, Walk	Decisions, Interviews

BLOCKS OF TIME (B1, B2...)

How can you put this idea into practice to make your day more effective? Break your work into blocks of time based on the type of work. For example, reserve a block for doing thinking work, another for meetings, and reserve time to do routine tasks like emails and responding to chats. As David Rock says "One big advantage of this strategy is that you can shift around the type of work you do, to let your brain recover. If you were doing physical exercise, you wouldn't do heavy lifting all day. You'd do some heavy lifting, then some cardiovascular exercise, and then some stretching. Each time you changed your exercise mode, your muscles would get used in new ways, with some resting while others worked. It's similar with mixing up types of thinking. Give your brain a rest when you can by mixing things up."[19] Simply put, dedicate your peak mental energy to tasks that demand it by scheduling them right.

So, next time you find yourself furious for not being able to solve a problem and slip into a fixed mindset thinking, simply ask yourself "Is it the best time of the day for you to solve it. Should you take a break and get back to it later today or maybe even tomorrow?"

"Mix it to fix it" is a growth mindset strategy that emphasizes the need to:

- Recharge your batteries by including breaks in your work.
- Schedule your work into different blocks of time based on the mental demands of work.

Knowing that your brain is so powerful and capable should inspire you to think about your own life. Are you doing things without really optimizing your brain for maximum effectiveness? Leverage the strategies in this chapter to get the best out of your time and energy. We all have a limited pool of energy and knowing how to spend it carefully can make a significant difference in the life we build for ourselves. In the next chapter, we will learn how to use mistakes and problems as opportunities to get better and not let temporary setbacks become permanent excuses to quit.

Chapter Summary

- Your brain is like a muscle that has the amazing ability to change, adapt and grow with practice. Exercising your body builds muscles, exercising your brain keeps it healthy and strong.
- With practice, you can be a little bit better every day. Maintaining consistency of action strengthens the circuits in your brain so that what was once difficult becomes automatic.
- Growth mindset can help you trigger the right behavior, but the only way to grow is to sustain action. You can't exercise your brain muscles by watching from the sidelines, you actually need to step into the arena and be part of the game.
- Effort matters, but it's the right kind of effort that matters more. If you aren't struggling, you aren't learning.
- The way you talk to yourself plays a key role in how you lead your life. Shifting from negative self-talk in the form of permanent and pervasive interpretations to positive self-talk in the form of temporary and specific explanations can help you take control of your life by gaining clarity and engaging in problem-solving instead of feeling hopeless and helpless about your situation.
- True change in mindset can happen only through an identity change. Get past labels and think about the behaviors and actions of the person you wish to become.
- Your unconscious mind is your superhero. Surround it with the same goals and cues that you want to pick up voluntarily. It will do its job behind the scenes for you.

- Being stuck on something does not signal your incompetence, it's an excuse to take a break. Give your fatigued brain some rest to allow it to function at its best.

CHAPTER 3

Get Comfortable With Mistakes

THERE'S IRONY in mistakes - contrary to the fact that mistakes sound bad, it's amusing to know they are good for us. As imperfect human beings, we all, at some point or the other, avoid taking responsibility for our actions and use blame, lies, and other excuses to ignore the consequences of our decisions. While most of us don't make life and death decisions and consequences of our mistakes are rather trivial than being tragic, at least in the larger scheme of things, we find it extremely hard to accept and say *"I made a mistake,"* first to ourselves and then to others. The choice to suck it up or not determines how we act and what we do next. Covering up mistakes instead of owning them is what leads to a tiff in couples, loss of trust between friends, unhealthy practices at work, and even stalls our own personal growth. How can we learn from our mistakes unless we admit that we made them in the first place?

Friedrich Nietzsche, a German philosopher once stated "What doesn't kill me, makes me stronger."[1] It conveys a simple fact - the path to success goes through failure. It's scattered with mistakes, big and small and when confronted with challenges, we emerge on the other side more confident than we began. But this belief is not for everyone and people with a fixed mindset don't buy into this idea. For them, mistake is not just a thing to be avoided, it's a thing to be avoided at all costs. This active focus on avoiding mistakes is a major factor into their decision-making process, often determining not only how they act but also how they react afterward.

Growth mindset people don't think this way. Neither do they actively chase mistakes nor obsess about avoiding them either. Mistake is just one component of their thinking, a necessary step to learn and grow. This creates a split in the middle with fixed mindset people on one side promoting "mistakes are bad" theory and growth mindset people on the other leading with "'mistakes are good."

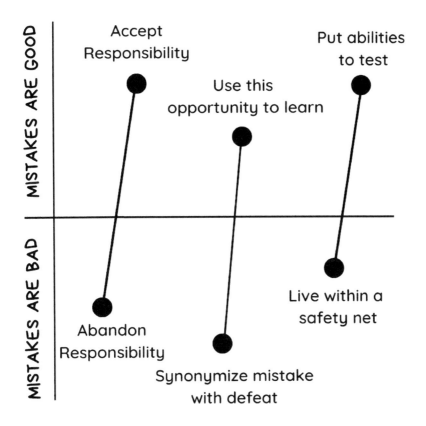

People in the "mistakes are bad" group:

1. Abandon their responsibility
2. Synonymize mistake with defeat
3. Live within a safety net

Abandon their responsibility

People who consider mistakes as bad live with a false sense of reality often blaming situations and environments beyond their control for their mistakes. Always some excuse for things not turning out the way they intended - at one time it was a coworker who screwed up the integration, another time they missed the deadline since the timeline was unrealistic, sometimes it's their children distracting them from focusing and a major cause for a calculation mistake on their report and at other times it's a system crash that ate into their precious time leaving them less time to prepare the presentation. Why spend time identifying their contribution to the mistake when someone else is the source of their problem?

Synonymize mistake with defeat

People with "mistakes are bad" theory feel great when things are going well but fall apart when things aren't. One mistake and they lose interest and drop out - they just don't want to look stupid. For them, mistakes aren't disappointing and temporary, they are powerful forces that pull them down from which they never quite recover, often telling themselves some version of *"I can never be good enough! I don't have what it takes! What's the point in trying if I will never succeed anyways!"* When mistakes do not align with their goal of proving their smartness and reflect badly on their competence, they hide them to avoid being criticized. Accepting mistakes is accepting defeat and that doesn't go quite so well with the image they have built for themselves.

Live within a safety net

What's more risky than doing something you have never done before? Fear of mistakes creates a strong desire to play safe. When evaluating opportunities, their inner voice tells them to stick to the known, do things they have always done before, avoid experimentation, ignore challenges and reject opportunities that are risky. Accepting mediocrity as the way of life since they never take steps to improve their skills. Constant vigilance to "avoid mistakes at all costs" leads to further stress and anxiety.

People in the "mistakes are good" group:
1. Accept responsibility
2. Use this experience to learn and grow
3. Put their abilities to test

Accept responsibility

Even though mistakes hurt and accepting a mistake is nothing but emotionally unpleasant, these people take complete responsibility for their mistakes. They refuse to engage in blame games, dig deeper to analyze their mistake, and identify what they could have done to prevent it. Hardly easy and pleasant, what keeps them going is knowing that finding the root cause of mistakes is the only way to avoid it in the future.

Use this experience to learn and grow

Mistakes are singular events that in no way reflect on their abilities or a measure of their competence. They are signals to try harder, implement better strategies and seek help. Missed a deadline? You probably need to put in more effort. Lost a deal? Try a different strategy next time. Nothings working out? Ask for help. With their decision rooted in learning and growth, when presented with evidence that confronts their point of view and highlights their mistake, they do not put on an armor of self-justification, but rather show curiosity to understand by saying *"I might be wrong. Let's review this together."*

Put their abilities to test

They are aware that the path to opportunities comes with its own challenges and they will make many mistakes along the way, but they cannot learn without putting themselves out there. Embracing difficulties and unknowns, brushing off the dust when they fall down, and moving ahead is the only way to build skills and abilities. Truth be told, they may not get what they set out to achieve, and yes, they might be disappointed for a brief period, but they soon bounce back with a dream of a better future. In their world, success is not a destination, it's a journey.

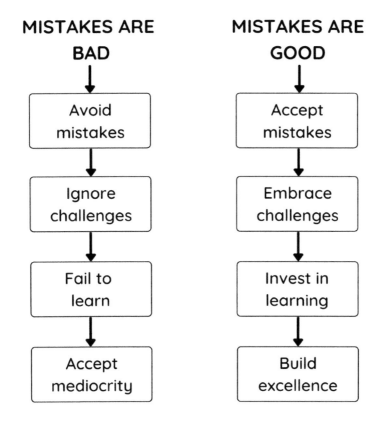

Now that you know about the two groups, let's do this small exercise. Take a moment to think about which group you belong to - do you identify yourself with the "mistakes are bad" or "mistakes are good" group? Which part of your thinking accentuates this belief? Be honest with yourself.

Your reaction to mistakes is in large part a factor of your environment as you are tempted into the ways of the people around you. Think for a moment - how do people around you respond to mistakes and failures? Do they encourage open discussions, ask questions and use humility and curiosity to get to the underlying cause or the blame game gets in the way of embracing failure lessons? Are you part of a culture where admitting mistakes means taking the blame? Do people around you practice openness, patience, and tolerance for mistakes?[2] How does your thinking align with people that are close to you?

It's easy to accept mistakes when no one is looking, but how do you act when others are around? Do you practice courage? Reminds me of John Wooden, the legendary UCLA basketball coach who was fond of saying "Success is never final; failure is never fatal. It's courage that counts."[3]

> 1st step = Update your belief system to "mistakes are good"

While the right belief is a necessary condition to make any significant change in your life, as we will see later in this chapter it's not sufficient. Even with the right belief, self-justification can get in the way. You may believe that "mistakes are good," but actually fail to put effective strategies for learning from your mistakes into practice.

DESTIGMATIZE MISTAKES: NOBODY IS PERFECT

N. Wayne Hale Jr. was launch integration manager at NASA in 2003, when seven astronauts died in the explosion of the space shuttle Columbia. In a letter to NASA employees, Hale took full responsibility for the disaster. He accepted his mistake:

"I had the opportunity and the information and I failed to make use of it. I don't know what an inquest or a court of law would say, but I stand condemned in the court of my own conscience to be guilty of not preventing the Columbia disaster. We could discuss the particulars: inattention, incompetence, distraction, lack of conviction, lack of understanding, a lack of backbone, laziness. The bottom line is that I failed to understand what I was being told; I failed to stand up and be counted. Therefore look no further; I am guilty of allowing Columbia to crash."[4] Even though a worker at Kennedy Space Center had complained to him that they hadn't heard any NASA managers admit to being at fault for the disaster, he said "I cannot speak for others but let me set my record straight. I am at fault."

He wrote in his letter "the nation has told us to get up, fix our shortcomings, fly again — and make sure it doesn't happen again. ... The nation is giving us another chance. Not just to fly the shuttle again, but to continue to explore the universe in our generation."

Once he got down to solving the cultural problems at NASA, he said "The first thing we've got to do is we've got to put the arrogance aside." Hale became a listener. When an engineer came to him with an issue after the accident, even if he didn't understand it, he tried. Hale oversaw many of the shuttle flights after the accident. It did not fail again. He says they made plenty of changes to checklists. But he thinks the biggest change was that everyone who worked at NASA became better at talking — and listening.[5] That's the power of acknowledging mistakes and learning from them.

In another astonishing event, Oprah Winfrey dedicated an entire show apologizing for making a mistake.[6]

A Million Little Pieces, published in 2003 was James Frey's memoir of drug addiction and recovery. Oprah Winfrey picked up the book for her popular on-air book club, an endorsement that boosted Frey's sales into millions as his memoir climbed the best sellers list. Later in October 2005, Frey appeared on "The Oprah Winfrey Show" to promote his book, which Oprah had previously said she "couldn't put down," calling it "a gut-wrenching memoir that is raw and it's so real." Then on January 8, 2006, The Smoking Gun website published that Frey had falsified and exaggerated many parts of his story. At first, Oprah justified her support for Frey when she called in to the "Larry King Live" show and said, "The underlying message of redemption in James Frey's memoir still resonates with me and I know that it resonates with millions of other people who have read this book, and will continue to read this book."

But later Oprah realized her mistake and took responsibility for it. She got Frey onto her show once again and started right off with an apology for her call to Larry King Live show "I regret that phone call," she said to her audience. "I made a mistake and I left the impression that the truth does not matter and I am deeply sorry about that because that is not what I believe. I called in because I love the message of this book and at the time and every day I was reading e-mail after e-mail from so many people who have been inspired by it. And, I have to say that I allowed that to cloud my judgment. And so to everyone who has challenged me on this issue of truth, you are absolutely right."

Later in the show, she even told Washington Post columnist Richard Cohen who had called Oprah "not only wrong, but deluded" that she was impressed with what he said, because "sometimes criticism can be very helpful. So thank you very much. You were right. I was wrong." Towards the end of the hour, the New York Times columnist Frank Rich appeared on the show to echo Richard Cohen, giving kudos to Oprah for speaking up, for taking a stand. "The hardest thing to do is admit a mistake," he said. Oprah eventually turned around and took responsibility for her actions and that matters too.

If Oprah and Hale could acknowledge their mistakes in front of millions of people, why can't we do it too? Mistakes are not terrible personal failings that need to be denied or justified, they are inevitable aspects of life that can help us grow. Repeat this every time you find yourself hiding from your mistakes.

2nd step = Acknowledge your mistake

Let's do one exercise. Think about any two successful people in your life you admire - it could be your friend, coworker, parents, teacher, coach, anyone. Now, reach out to them and discuss their path to success. What mistakes did they make along the way, how difficult was the experience, how they felt in those moments, what did they do afterward, and what were their learnings? Once you have the information, write it down using the template below and use it as a reminder that even successful people make mistakes. Use it as a source of inspiration to do the right thing for yourself.

Exercise: Mistakes can inspire

My inspiration #1 _____

1. What mistake did they make?

   _____

   _____

2. What did they learn?

   _____

   _____

3. How can I apply this in my own life?

_____

_____

My inspiration #2 _____

1. What mistake did they make?

_____

_____

2. What did they learn?

_____

_____

3. How can I apply this in my own life?

_____

_____

You can download a printable version of "Mistakes Can Inspire" at: techtello.com/upgrade-your-mindset/templates/

BREAK IT DOWN: WHAT'S UNDER YOUR CONTROL

Not all mistakes are created equal and not all mistakes are desirable. Some mistakes evoke feelings of embarrassment, shock, and confusion, others can be good for us, and a few can also be disastrous, often hurting and harming others by destroying the trust they placed in us. We place too much focus on unavoidable mistakes that are beyond our control while letting the ones with tremendous growth opportunities slip by. Mistakes that do catch our attention fail to generate any value since we refuse to use a proper lens to analyze them. By treating all mistakes equal, we fail to take proper action.

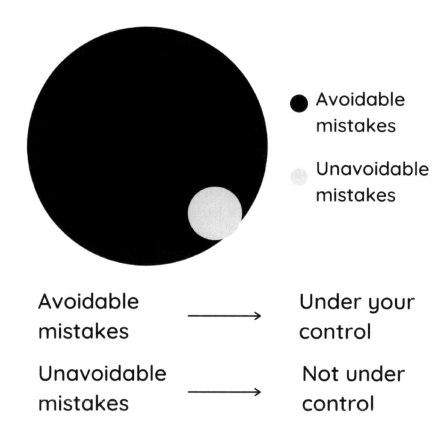

| Avoidable mistakes | → | Under your control |
| Unavoidable mistakes | → | Not under control |

Mistakes are either avoidable - within your control, or unavoidable - driven by external circumstances beyond your reach or a by-product of learning something new. Knowing this distinction can help you decide the next best possible course of action.

Let's explore avoidable mistakes first. Avoidable mistakes are clear indicators of how certain behaviors can have a damaging effect on your relationships, work, and your growth. Once you learn to recognize these behaviors, you can implement corrective actions to avoid these mistakes in the future. Let's say being the financial expert in the house, you decide to invest a small portion of your wealth, but despite being extremely cautious you lose it all. At worst, you will feel embarrassed by it. Now, imagine doing the same thing with your parent's money. This time instead of placing a small bet, you invest their life savings. How would you feel? What will be their reaction? When dealing with high-stakes situations, risk-taking behaviors aren't really opportunities for learning and whenever possible, it's better to prevent them than to be sorry.

Another great opportunity lies in observing your own behavior when you know how to do something well. Excessive confidence in your abilities can distract you from focussing on the task at hand. You may start taking things casually. Aren't these great opportunities to fix your behavior and avoid making a mistake in the first place?

- You may procrastinate for a long time and then rush through the presentation at the last moment.
- You may not pay attention to the details of your marketing pitch and implement the same old strategies that have always worked for you even though the situation demands a new one.
- You may refuse to fact-check the assertions in your editorial.

Unavoidable mistakes demand a completely different orientation. Do you fret about the part of the mistake that was beyond your control? Could you have done anything to change your situation? Epictetus, a Greek Stoic philosopher once wrote "In life our first job is this, to divide and distinguish things into two categories: externals I cannot control, but the choices I make with regard to them I do control."[7] Instead of focussing on the part of the mistake you couldn't control, look inwardly to the decisions you made. Say you organized an open-air event and a huge downpour at the last minute turned it into a disaster for the organizers and the attendees alike.

Would you continue to blame the weather or use it as learning to have a backup plan for your next event?

Another type of unavoidable mistake happens when you are trying to expand your abilities, build new skills, or acquire new knowledge. Since you don't know how to do something well yet, you are bound to make some errors. Every mistake serves as a positive signal that you are challenging and pushing your boundaries to learn something new, often implying that you are headed in the right direction. These mistakes are good, unavoidable, and necessary for your growth. As Ed Catmull, co-founder of Pixar and president of Walt Disney Animation Studios puts it "Failure isn't a necessary evil. In fact, it isn't evil at all. It is a necessary consequence of doing something new."[8]

3rd step = Categorize your mistake

If you keep pushing all your mistakes into the same pile, you will never learn anything from them. Ask yourself these questions to see mistakes for what they are and learn from their unique insights:

1. Did I show risky behavior in a high stake situation?
2. Is my sloppiness contributing to all these mistakes?
3. Are these mistakes a result of my desire to learn something new?
4. Did an external factor beyond my control contributed to this mistake?

RECOGNIZE NEGATIVITY: DENIAL AND SELF-JUSTIFICATION

Most people think of learning from mistakes as a three-step process:

1. Acknowledge the mistake
2. Reflect on what went wrong and assimilate it into easy-to-implement strategies
3. Put these strategies to action

Easy-peasy lemon squeezy. Not so much. It's more complicated than that. Acknowledging a mistake is simply an acknowledgment of its existence. You haven't really accepted your part in it yet. It's the reflection stage where you try to make sense of everything that happened and it's exactly where reality goes up for distortion. Usually, when you make a mistake and either recognize it yourself or it's brought to your attention, you feel an emotion - anger, fear, sadness, embarrassment, disappointment, hopelessness, anxiety, frustration, or curiosity, and then you try to rationalize that emotion. You give it a language by telling yourself a story, often rationalizing how you see the various events unfold.

When your extreme reaction to mistakes is as author Kathryn Schulz describes in her book *Being Wrong* "you wish yourself out of existence. You describe the moment of realization as wanting to crawl into a cave, fall through a hole in the floor, or simply disappear. You talk about losing face as if your mistake really did cause you to disappear-as if your identity was rubbed out by the experience of being wrong,"[9] you latch onto self-doubt to hide from your mistakes: *"I feel small compared to others!" "I am worried about what others will think about me!" "I don't want to look incompetent!"*

"I don't want to be criticized!" "I am not confident in my abilities!" "I am scared of failing!"

SELF DOUBT
I am scared of failing
I am not confident in my abilities
I don't want to be criticized
I don't want to look incompetent
I just want to raise my self-esteem
I feel small compared to others
I am worried what others will think about me

With the goal of protecting your self-esteem, self-justification automatically springs to action helping you get rid of negative emotions. Elliot Aronson, a social psychologist, describes self-justification as "lying to ourselves."[10] He adds "Self-justification not only minimizes our mistakes and bad decisions; it is also the reason that everyone can see a hypocrite in action except the hypocrite. That is why self-justification is more powerful and more dangerous than the explicit lie. It allows people to convince themselves that what they did was the best thing they could have done. In fact, come to think of it, it was the right thing." Since self-justification works beneath consciousness, you may not even realize that you are using it as a shield by shunning your responsibility: *I didn't make a mistake!* Self-justification protects you by blaming something or someone else for your situation.

- I missed a deadline because it was unrealistic. At least I tried my best.
- I ate unhealthy food yesterday because my roommate bought a lot of junk food. Really, there were no better options.
- I crashed into a car because the other driver was reckless. I actually prevented much bigger damage.
- I need to stick to my career even though it makes me miserable because I have spent so much time and energy on it. There aren't better jobs out there.

When you justify your actions to others, there's still a possibility of correction since the other person might point it out. But when you justify it to yourself, believing your version as the truth, there's no chance of self-correction or learning. You get stuck in your own mistake loop, reinforcing the beliefs you hold and strengthening your lies with every mistake you commit. It blocks your ability to see your own mistakes by distorting reality and blocking the information you need to see issues clearly. How can you ever learn and grow when you can't even admit your own mistakes?

Does this mean there's no hope for you? Absolutely not. You can learn to break this loop as we will see in the next section but first, you need to accept it exists. We all, at some point or the other, fall for self-justification and use it as an escape route for covering our mistakes.

4th step = Recognize the mistake loop

Let's do this exercise. Think of any recent mistake where you refused to take responsibility - what was the mistake, how did you feel when you first learnt about the mistake (think of the emotion), what story did you tell yourself, did the rationalization reinforced your belief? Draw out your own mistake loop and add as many details as possible in the resource provided below.

It's important that you do this exercise now as we will learn to break this loop in the next section.

Exercise: The mistake loop

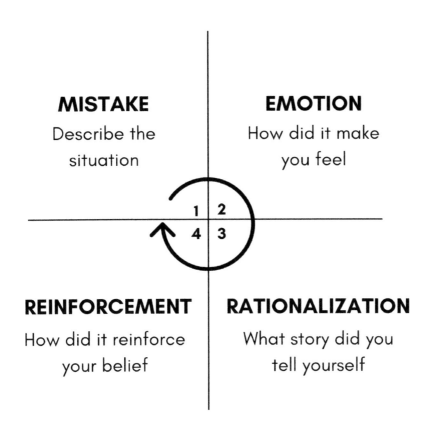

You can download a printable version of "The Mistake Loop" at:
techtello.com/upgrade-your-mindset/templates/

REFRAME REALITY: LETTING GO AND OWNING UP

Seeking an external perspective on our mistakes doesn't really help much. Hardly anyone knows the reality of our situation, most won't speak up to avoid hurting us, some will give us irrelevant advice and very few will dare to speak the truth. We don't fail to see reality because of lack of information. The problem is with how we make decisions. We collect bits and pieces of information that confirm our thinking and reject every piece of evidence that contradicts it. Given an opportunity to present itself, self-justification is really good at its job. It won't budge once you let it in by ignoring any outside information that interferes with its own conclusion. The only way to break out of this loop of mistake followed by self-justification, followed by further reinforcement is to nip it in the bud. Being attentive to your own thinking and catching yourself before it's too late.

Instead of letting automatic thinking drive your decision, you can learn to recognize these moments of discomfort and make a conscious choice to prevent them from clouding your judgment. You can break the loop by stopping right at the moment when you feel an emotion and inserting a moment of self-declaration. What do you need to do? Cut the cord, don't let rationalization kick in. Grab it at its source and deny it the power to justify your actions.

How? The moment you feel an emotion, acknowledge your mistake and accept responsibility. Repeat this to yourself multiple times "I made a mistake. I can learn from it." This simple phrase will empower your mind to adopt a solutioning mode instead of a self-defeating goal of pushing blame externally. With a new goal, you will no longer look backward with dissatisfaction, you will look forward with the desire to grow. You will experience a different spin on the negative emotions as you become the writer of your own story.

5th step = Break the loop

Real work starts now. Analyzing your mistake won't be an easy task. No doubt, the exercise will be unpleasant. The experience is nothing but emotionally draining and it's easy to get carried away by emotions - attaching superficial causes or speeding through the analysis without any significant conclusions. Don't let that happen. Shift from obvious and superficial reasons to the underlying root cause. Dig in, draw connections, identify and learn from your past, ask questions and only accept an answer that clarifies what you did wrong and what action could have prevented the mistake from happening - what went wrong, why did you make the mistake, was the mistake avoidable or unavoidable, how can you fix it, what does this mistake teach you about yourself?

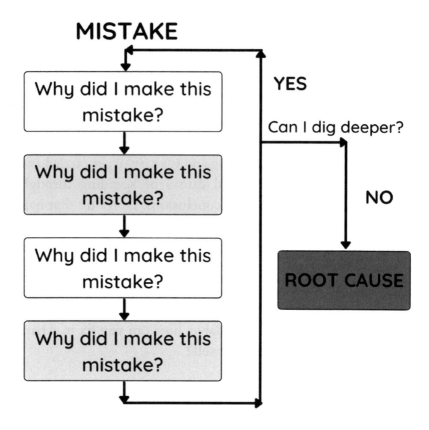

A powerful technique to go from superficial understanding of your mistake to the underlying root cause is to use the "five whys" technique[11] designed by Sakichi Toyoda who used it within the Toyota Motor Corporation during the evolution of its manufacturing methodologies. Ask why the mistake occurred and use the answer as the premise for the next question repeating this whole process five times to dig deeper into the actual cause of the issue. By repeating "why" five times, the nature of the problem and its solution becomes clear. Consider this example:

1. Q: "Why did I take longer than expected to deliver on the project?" A: I had to rework on some of the features.
2. Q: "Why did I need to rework on some features?" A: I made wrong assumptions about certain requirements.
3. Q: "Why did I make wrong assumptions about these requirements?" A: I did not clarify the requirements at the beginning.
4. Q: "Why did I not clarify the requirements in the beginning?" A: I waited too long to start work and then assumed it was too late to ask any clarifying questions.
5. Q: "Why did I wait too long to start work?" A: I was overconfident in my abilities.

This example clearly demonstrates that the actual mistake is quite different from the answer to the first question. Without digging deeper, we might stop at the first answer that comes to our mind. Hardly the answer we need to solve the problem and prevent it from occurring again. Five whys is a general guideline. You can stop at three or go all the way till seven whys, whatever gets you the answer you need to understand your mistake better.

6th step = Learn from your mistake

The exercise may be unpleasant, but the results are marvelous. A little pain turns into a lot of gain in the future and honestly, it's much easier to solve a mistake you just made instead of dealing with it once it has become too big to manage. As Elliot Aronson says "If you can admit a mistake when it is the size of an acorn, it is easier to repair than when it has become the size of a tree, with deep, wide-ranging roots."[12]

Hopefully, this will set your thinking in motion for the mistakes you have made in your own life. Repeat the exercise we did in the

90 UPGRADE YOUR MINDSET

previous section. This time instead of repeating the loop, break it using the strategies specified here. Use the resource provided below to learn from your mistakes.

Exercise: Learning from mistakes

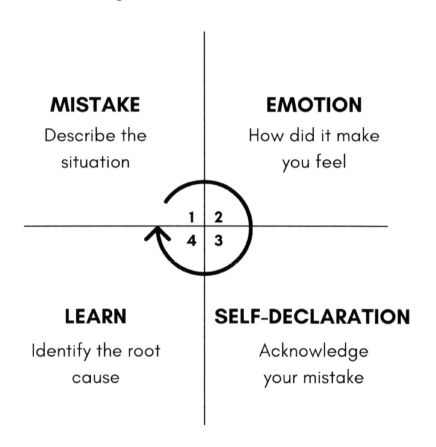

You can download a printable version of "Learning from Mistakes" at:
techtello.com/upgrade-your-mindset/templates/

How do you feel after this exercise? Could you have learnt this much without making a mistake?

If you do this every time you make a mistake, you can get so much better at doing things. You can learn and grow.

REMIND YOURSELF: YOU AREN'T ALONE

Ask successful people how they have achieved success in life and you will often find an expression of the importance of mistakes in shaping up their lives. People who are at the top of their game don't have everything figured out. They still make plenty of mistakes. There are times when they struggle. What makes them stand out from others is not their setbacks, but their willingness to use their mistakes to push forward.

When in doubt, always remember, nobody is perfect. Everyone has a pencil and an eraser, a pencil to write their own life, and an eraser to fix the parts they don't like. Because really, only you can.

Do this last exercise on mistakes. Read each of the quotes below and write down what each one means to you. You can also do this as a group exercise with your team or friends and share how each one of you thinks. Doing it together is not only more fun, but it's also a lot more learning by getting a peek into so many unique perspectives.

Exercise: Everyone makes mistakes

1. "Anyone who has never made a mistake has never tried anything new." —— Albert Einstein

2. "Good judgment comes from experience, and experience comes from bad judgment." —— Rita Mae Brown

3. "Freedom is not worth having if it does not include the freedom to make mistakes." —— Mahatma Gandhi

4. "The greatest mistake you can make in life is to be continually fearing you will make one." —— Elbert Hubbard

5. "You must never feel badly about making mistakes ... as long as you take the trouble to learn from them. For you often learn more by being wrong for the right reasons than you do by being right for the wrong reasons." —— Norton Juster

6. "All of us have hard decisions to make at times in our lives; not all of them will be right, and not all of them will be wise. Some are complicated, with consequences we could never have foreseen. If we can resist the temptation to justify our actions in a rigid, overconfident way, we can leave the door open to empathy and an appreciation of life's complexity, including the possibility that what was right for us might not have been right for others." —— Elliot Aronson

You can download a printable version of "Everyone Makes Mistakes" at:
techtello.com/upgrade-your-mindset/templates/

I am sure you will continue to make plenty of mistakes in your life, there's no getting around it. But now, instead of engaging in behaviors that push you back, you will choose to accept responsibility and move forward. You will be willing to go through unpleasant experiences in the moment to have far better experiences in the future. You will make the right choices even if they are painful at first because only you know the joy they bring afterwards. You will simply refuse to hide behind a fixed mindset and embrace the freedom to make mistakes with a growth mindset.

In the next chapter, we will learn about the incredible power of the simple word "yet," how doing anything significant requires more than one attempt and the strategies to overcome our blind spots to make meaningful progress.

Chapter Summary

- Mistakes are not terrible personal failings that need to be justified. They don't reflect on your stupidity or incompetence. Use them as valuable signals to learn and grow.
- Everyone makes mistakes in life. What differs is their reaction. People who hide behind their mistakes choose a life of mediocrity, while those who accept responsibility lead with curiosity.
- All mistakes are not equal. Avoidable mistakes are tremendous growth opportunities often hidden in plain sight. Unavoidable mistakes are an essential part of learning something new.
- Don't just acknowledge a mistake, accept responsibility. Seeing the mistake for what it is isn't easy as it requires going around your own cognitive biases.
- Don't let the siren song of self-justification make you believe in your own lies and prevent you from accepting the reality of your situation. Curb it at its roots.
- Accept your mistakes. It will empower your mind to adopt a solutioning mode instead of a self-defeating goal of pushing blame externally.

- Move from a superficial understanding of the problem to the underlying root cause. That's where growth lies.

CHAPTER 4

Apply Incredible Power of Yet

WHEN MY daughter Myra, soon to be 8 years old, comes to me saying: *I can't skate down the slopes! I can't do this dance move! I can't fix this toy car!* I simply ask her to complete the sentence with "yet" - *I can't skate down the slopes yet! I can't do this dance move yet! I can't fix this toy car yet!* Saying "I can't do" triggers a belief that she can never do it, it's not within her reach. That makes her give up without trying hard enough. Saying "I can't do...yet" signals she just can't do it right now, but it's always learnable. With more effort or better strategy, it's achievable. One is about accepting defeat, the other is about embracing the challenge.

There's another big difference between "I can't do" and "I can't do yet." *I can't* is the feeling of being stuck in the present, not good enough right now. *I can't yet* is about the vision, the motivation to improve in the future. It's what Mark Gibson, a former member of the British National team who has been coaching kids since 1982 describes is the difference between winners and whiners. He says "The winners will create a long list of things they must do to learn the skill they want. I must learn to cast to handstand correctly. I must develop an efficient tap swing through the bottom. I must form a tight kick over the bar. Your whiners, on the other hand, will get busy creating a long list of excuses to justify their self-doubt. I'm a lousy caster. I can't tap swing. I get scared when I'm upside-down. In other words your winners are forming a plan of action while the whiners are driving their roots of mediocrity deeper and deeper."[1]

I can't do this...yet.
This doesn't work...yet.
I don't know...yet.
It doesn't make sense...yet.
I don't get it...yet.
I'm not good at this...yet.

"Yet."

This simple three-letter word is the sound of possibility, a positive intervention in our life to help us see straight. The nudge we all need to take control of our life by looking beyond the obstacles in the present to the opportunities of tomorrow. "Yet" carries with it the expectation that we can reach our destination. It creates an excitement into the future about all the incredible things we can't do yet. Human beings are naturally inclined to learn with a lifelong capacity for new ways of thinking and new ways of doing things.[2] The sound of yet reinforces that curiosity. It reminds us that we may not be good enough yet, skilled enough yet and that intimidating thing staring down at us may scare the hell out of us, but it's definitely within our reach. It may take a little longer, but we can get to it only if we try hard enough and long enough.

Seth Godin describes "yet" as a simple missing word. He says "Yet isn't the result of brazen persistence. It's what we earn with learning, insight and generosity. Along the way, Yet turns can't into haven't. You can append it after any sentence related to your journey of achievement and contribution.

I haven't finished the project
I haven't learned how to juggle
I haven't made the sale
YET."[3]

This is the power of yet.

As this New York Times article points out, "If you've ever picked up a crossword puzzle and said to yourself, "I am not smart enough" or "I don't have a big enough vocabulary for this," here's a little secret: A crossword puzzle is not a test of intelligence, and solving is not really about the size of your vocabulary. Becoming a good solver is about understanding what the clues are asking you to do."[4] You may not know how to solve a crossword puzzle yet. But, you can absolutely learn to do that.

This applies to everything. You aren't born with all the skills you need in life, you have to work hard to build them. Can't drive a car yet? You can learn to drive it. Can't seal a deal yet? You can learn to negotiate better. Can't shoot a hoop yet? You can learn to shoot hoops better. When your fixed mindset wants to give up with "I can't do," use your growth mindset to correct it with "I can't do…yet." Yet with "what next" thinking can turn the obstacles in your path upside down. It can make possible that which didn't seem possible earlier. It can show you a way out or another path to where you need to go.

- You haven't failed in a task, you just haven't succeeded…yet.
- You don't give up when you don't know the answer, you just haven't found the answer…yet.
- You don't quit with an attitude of "it can't be done," you persist with "I just haven't figured it out…yet."

Keep searching for ways to get better, to improve, to change your situation. There's a chance you might find them. Give up and stop searching. I can guarantee you won't find a thing. Yet signals hope - a little voice in our head that tells us to not give up, to fight whatever obstacles stand in our way, to be creative with new strategies instead of feeling frustrated about what doesn't work, to consider mistakes and failures as a sign of progress, to dream bigger, better and to make that dream possible. Because anything is possible only when we believe it is.

IS THERE SOMETHING YOU CAN'T DO YET?

There are so many things you want to know,
So many ways you want to grow,
There are so many things you want to be,
So many milestones you want to see.

You will get there if you never forget
The superpower of the word, YET!

When you first tried to talk, you were hard to understand,
When you first tried to eat, you needed a hand.
When you first tried to walk, you fell and fell,
When you first tried to run, it didn't go well.

But your baby self knew something we often forget
The superpower of the word YET!

Somehow you knew that if you kept trying

> Your chances of success would keep multiplying.
> The same is true with every risk that you take,
> You just have to learn from every mistake.
>
> Where you put your effort, the goal will be met
> As long as you remember the superpower of YET!
>
> By Heidi Harrell[5]

This beautiful poem by Heidi reminds me of childhood - that little spark of joy we got when we mastered a new skill, learnt something new, or accomplished a goal. Where's that spark now? When did we stop believing as adults? It's not that we don't have potential. We have plenty of it. Yet, we do nothing to utilize it. We are too scared to try, paralyzed by fear, anxious of our failures, stressed about our results, and reluctant to put in the effort. Often tangled in the nitty-gritties of life, we let multiple opportunities slip by. Even with all the professional frustration and unmet expectations, we choose to feel helpless - too stubborn to update our beliefs, too busy to invest in our skills, and too awkward about our failures - no wonder, we label ourselves as failures or our goals as impossible.

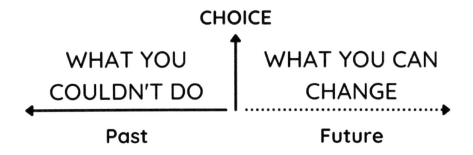

Nothing is going to change unless you take responsibility and ownership, unless you are willing to break things apart, unless you learn to iterate, unless you become tolerant to mistakes, unless you decide to go all the way or as Epictetus said "persist and resist"[6] - persist in your effort and resist the easy path to give up.

You are capable of a lot more than you perceive yourself to be. Spend less time worrying, more time doing. Less time in being right, more time in doing the right thing. Less time in proving yourself, more time in learning something new. Less time treading water, more time learning how to climb steep slopes.

Let's do this exercise. Is there something you don't have a lot of experience with or a thing you don't know how to solve yet? What are some of the problems you are facing? Anything you would like to change about yourself? These are all great opportunities to build skills that will help you in the future. Make a list of things you "can't do yet" that you would like to learn or "don't do well yet" that you would like to improve. Now, write them down. Don't forget to put "yet" at the end of each sentence.

Exercise: I can't do yet / I don't do well yet

What is it I can't do yet or don't do well yet?

1. _____

2. _____

3. _____

4. _____

5. _____

You can download a printable version of "I Can't Do Yet / I Don't Do Well Yet" at:
techtello.com/upgrade-your-mindset/templates/

Once the list is ready, pick any one skill or activity from the list to start and apply the strategies in the rest of this chapter. Continue to put into practice what you learnt earlier about mistakes. Remember, a good part of doing anything new is acknowledging mistakes and using them to improve.

TRY IT ONE MORE TIME

Thomas Edison said "Our greatest weakness lies in giving up. The most certain way to succeed is always to try just one more time."

How many times have you tried to achieve something, but then gave up only after a handful of attempts? Why did you not get the desired outcomes?

Maybe you didn't put in the effort.

Maybe you didn't try hard enough.

Maybe you didn't dedicate enough time.

Maybe you didn't learn from your mistakes.

Maybe you were looking for an easy way out.

Maybe you were distracted.

What if you had tried just one more time with complete dedication, real focus, time, and energy required to solve it? Do you think you could have succeeded?

Thomas Edison's teachers said he was "too stupid to learn anything." He was fired from his first two jobs for being non-productive. It took him 1,000 unsuccessful attempts (and maybe even more) to invent the light bulb. When a reporter asked, "How did it feel to fail 1,000 times?" Edison replied, "I didn't fail 1,000 times. The light bulb was an invention with 1,000 steps."[7]

The Wright brothers took years to invent the world's first successful motor-operated airplane. Why did the Wright brothers succeed when others failed?

Between 1899 to 1905, they conducted multiple experiments that led to the first successful powered airplane in 1903 and a refined, practical flying machine two years later.[8] Talking about the intensity of the problem, an article in Scientific American points out "The art of flying was a complicated dance between man, machine and air that required thousands of hours of practice to perfect."[9] Wilbur, one of the brothers said "It is the complexity of the flying problem that makes it so difficult. It is not . . . solved by stumbling upon a secret, but by the patient accumulation of information upon a hundred different points."[10]

What about Michael Jordan, the greatest basketball player of all time? Did success come to him easily? He was cut from his varsity basketball team during his sophomore year in high school and instead asked to play on the junior varsity team. Failure and disappointment didn't stop him.[11] He used them to be better. He played and worked himself to the limit. It was his relentless drive that led him to break numerous records and become the most decorated player in the history of the NBA. These famous quotes from Micahel Jordan himself describe the spirit with which he played.

"I visualized where I wanted to be, what kind of player I wanted to become. I knew exactly where I wanted to go, and I focused on getting there."

"I've missed more than 9000 shots in my career. I've lost almost 300 games. 26 times, I've been trusted to take the game winning shot and missed. I've failed over and over and over again in my life. And that is why I succeed."

"I don't do things half-heartedly. Because I know if I do, then I can expect half-hearted results."

Thomas Edison, Wright brothers, Michael Jordan, and numerous others who have achieved success have one thing in common - they didn't give up easily. They knew that doing anything significant requires more than one attempt. They changed their relationship with failure - iterating, failing, learning, and improving along the way. After all, when you try so many times and fail at something, you are not a failure. You now know for sure what doesn't work. It's a subtle shift in mindset, but an important one distinguishing between people who benefit from failure and those who don't because they refuse to listen, learn and change.

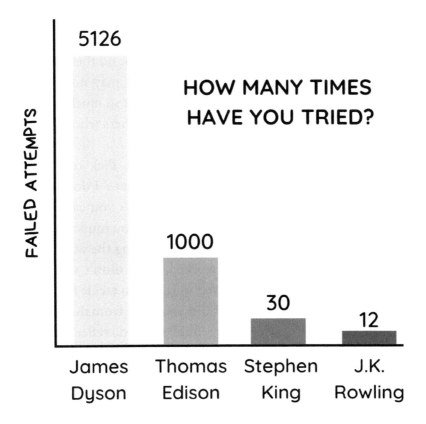

What if you also adopted that attitude? Not everything you do will require hundreds of hours and thousands of attempts.

Mastering a skill may take years, but you can get pretty good at anything within just a few weeks or a few months with the right kind of attitude. Don't rush through change, sustain action over time. Be determined to stick with the path until you reach your designated finish line. If you're not there yet, believe you will. Experiment! Try! Don't be afraid to get back to the drawing board, erase an answer that didn't work, imagine a new strategy or implement a different practice.

Yes, the experience will be frustrating at times. It will leave you feeling uncomfortable. Even bitter with the pain of not moving forward. Feel those emotions, but don't let them stop you from trying just one more time. Success may be just around the corner and maybe not. Eventually, nothing may work. You may not get what you want. The good part is you would have learnt so much along the way that it would set you apart from so many others who refused to even try or gave up too soon.

It's time to put this learning into practice. Pick one skill or activity from the previous exercise "I can't do yet / I don't do well yet." Now, think about three different strategies you can apply to improve that skill or complete that activity. As you implement these strategies, take time to capture your learnings along the way. Write in as much detail as possible - what worked, what didn't work, what challenges did you face, how prepared were you to tackle them, what mistakes did you commit, and what did you learn from them.

Once all the three strategies are implemented, reflect back and decide the next course of action - your next step. Does one of these strategies seem more promising? Should you continue investing in one of them or need a completely new strategy? Now that you are more experienced, can you foresee certain obstacles and be better prepared to handle them up front? Write them down in the same template.

Organizing your thoughts in this manner will not only help you bring into focus what you need to do to build the skill or complete the activity, but it will also help you stay realistic about the course you need to take to reach there. Instead of procrastinating and waiting for the perfect solution, you can now act and refine as you go forward. Instead of worrying about failing, you now know that setbacks are always expected and never permanent. Instead of being blocked by the obstacles in your path, you can devise new ways to where you need to go. Everything seems possible - confidence can curb your doubts and curiosity can lead you to discovery.

Don't waste time wishing or daydreaming, spend time making it a reality. Because you can. You just haven't started...yet. You can apply this practice to develop any new skills or for solving any problem you are facing.

Exercise: More than one attempt

1. What do I want to learn or what activity do I need to complete?

   _____

   _____

2. Where do I stand right now?

   _____

   _____

3. What's my first strategy to improve?

_____

_____

4. What did I learn from implementing this strategy?

_____

_____

5. What's my second strategy to improve?

_____

_____

6. What did I learn from implementing this strategy?

_____

_____

7. What's my third strategy to improve?

_____

_____

8. What did I learn from implementing this strategy?

_____

9. After trying multiple strategies, where do I stand now? What should I do next?

_____

_____

You can download a printable version of "More Than One Attempt" at:
techtello.com/upgrade-your-mindset/templates/

ASK FOR HELP

Growing up in a culture that promotes independence and individualization, it can be uncomfortable and quite embarrassing to admit "you need help." Not reaching out when you need help or not realizing that you even need one is the hallmark of a fixed mindset. Worrying about how others will perceive you and trying hard to maintain the image you have created for yourself can prevent you from drawing support from the people around you, exactly the kind of support you need to make progress.

Look at the last question in the previous exercise "More than one attempt" again. While answering it, did you consider asking for help? Did you think about who else might be useful to give you advice or help you strategize better? Why not?

Is it because you worry that asking for help will make you look weak or incompetent? Others will think less of you if they find you dependent. Does it make you question your own abilities?

Uncertainty of the outcome, risk of rejection, fear of looking vulnerable or appearing needy, and anxiety of diminished status is a very real feeling. But, you don't have to give in to this feeling. You can learn to challenge it by using your growth mindset. With the right strategies, you can look past your fears and increase your chance of getting just the help you need to move forward. You can change your hardwiring that connects independence to the ability to do everything on your own.

Making progress does not mean working on your own, it also requires working with others. Others can help you see what you are otherwise not able to see. Some of the most admired and successful people in the world do this: they constantly ask for help. They embrace discomfort to get to the information they need, ask questions to clarify their thinking, and show curiosity in learning from others. In a speech addressed to students, Barack Obama said "Don't be afraid to ask questions. Don't be afraid to ask for help when you need it. I do that every day. Asking for help isn't a sign of weakness, it's a sign of strength. It shows you have the courage to admit when you don't know something, and to learn something new."[12]

Isn't that true? Asking for help is indeed a sign of strength. It signals self-awareness of our limitations, humility to accept what we don't know, and the courage to ask for it. More than anything, it's a sign of confidence - confidence in our abilities to tackle whatever is standing in our way to get to where we need to go. The real risk isn't receiving criticism, facing rejection, or sounding foolish. It's not finding your way to the advice you need to move forward. Staying where you are because you refuse to break out of the mould. Don't let your fixed mindset take up the driver's seat. Check your ego at the door, stop acting awkward or feeling guilty. Just ask for help. You haven't finished what you started...yet.

Now to the real part: Actually asking for help. Since we have never been formally taught how to ask for help properly, know there's a process to it. Yes, there's a right and wrong way of asking for help! It's a four-step process:

1. Explicitly ask for it
2. State it as you need it
3. Put it into action
4. Share your learning

Ask	State	Act	Learn
1	2	3	4
Say it out loud	Be specific and direct	Plan for execution	Share your learnings

Explicitly ask for it

Are you standing around waiting for others to notice your need and then offer help? Trust me, it's not going to happen. You are not going to get any help unless you explicitly ask for it. Research shows that the illusion of transparency makes us believe our thoughts, needs, and feelings are as obvious to others as they are to us.[13] The truth is people are not mind readers and our need for help is less obvious to others. It's obvious to us. Not so much to anyone else. You have to let people know you need help. You have to actually ask for it.

Finding the right person to seek advice is a little bit of work. Don't fall for the excuse and quit - people around me can't really help. They don't understand what I need. It's an escape route. You haven't really put in the effort to get the help you need. Tap into your network - activate your weak links, reach out to your dormant ties. Don't assume they won't be helpful or they won't help. Frank Flynn, associate professor of organizational behavior at Stanford GSB states "People are more willing to help than you think, and that can be important to know when you're trying to get the resources you need to get a job done, when you're trying to solicit funds, or what have you."[14] We dramatically underestimate how likely others are to help us.

State it as you need it

Heidi Grant, a social psychologist says that it's a terrible idea to say "would love to get together and catch up" or "let's chat" or "let's connect over coffee" or "want to pick your brain" when you need help. It's clear people have an agenda that they don't want to share right away. She says "such vague requests are just terrible."[15] She advises to be specific and direct - state what you want and why you want it. "I would like to work together on this project" or "I would like to connect to get your advice" or "I need your help on…" You want to make it easy for the other person to listen to your problem and then decide if they can offer help or how they can be effective. When you make the request too vague, too broad or keep it too open-ended, others hesitate to help or end up giving advice that's not really useful.

Don't use phrases that make the conversation unproductive. Saying things like *"I feel terrible asking you for this"* or *"I don't normally ask for help"* trivializes the request and makes it unnecessary. Think for a moment about how it will make the other person feel. Why should they help you if you feel so bad about it? Using statements that make the other person feel trapped are the worst - *It's just this tiny thing! May I ask you a favor!* You haven't really stated what you want and expect the other person to jump enthusiastically and say "yes." To make it easy for the other person to say yes, you have to actually state the problem. If you find it hard to get to the point right away, a better conversation starter is to set the context. Something like "I have been struggling with [this] problem for the last few days. Being an expert in this field, I was hoping to get your advice on how I can move forward. Would you have some time to discuss the problem in detail?"

Maybe they will agree even when your request was vague, cryptic, and seemed unnecessary. But how are you sure they will give you the assistance you need? You didn't really leave them much choice to make the right decision - can I be useful, do I have the information this person needs, will I have the time, is there someone else who might be better suited to help out? Feeling trapped by their commitment, there will be no real motivation to solve your problem. Result - half-hearted conversations, quick patchy solutions, anything to seal the deal and get going.

Give them the information. Let them make a decision. When they sign up knowing fully well what they are getting into, they will be much more likely to assist you in the best possible manner. And if they do reject, stay positive and be understanding. Move on to someone else. Don't take it personally. Everyone has a bazillion things to do and you may not be their priority at the moment. Finally, state your request in person. Don't use email or chat or a message. You are thirty times more likely to get a "yes."[16]

Put it into action

Got the advice? Yay!! Now, act on it. If you don't agree with it, say so. Just because someone gave you the advice, doesn't mean you need to comply with it. Most people find it healthy to have disagreements and don't expect you to do everything they suggest. Put forward your viewpoint, discuss why it doesn't connect with you, and explore other alternatives. Just don't let it hang. Don't sit on it. Nothing's going to change if you do nothing. It's also disrespectful to the person who gave you their time.

Don't use delaying tactics either - I will do it someday. It's never going to happen. Good excuses will find their way to delay the thing that you fear, aren't sure about, or simply require some effort on your part. Commit to a plan - exactly when, where, and how are you going to put this advice into action. Don't make a daily decision. Set it up on your calendar. When it pops out, know it's time to act.

Share your learning

People who gave you their valuable time by helping you with your problem want to know the impact they created. It's what motivates them to help. No one wants to offer help and not know how it turned out. Be grateful for their advice even if it didn't work out. Share your learnings with them - Did your actions create the results you intended? What worked? What didn't work? What challenges did you face?

By explaining and sharing this information, not only will your skills improve, but you might also find new information through moments of self-reflection. You can draw useful connections between your actions and outcomes. You can find patterns that explain why a certain thing turned out the way it did. You can identify information that can be useful for preventing a failure from happening again. There are endless possibilities to what you might learn.

Appreciate the experience even if you don't achieve the desired outcome as it will be useful to implement better strategies in the future. Don't stop after the first failure. Conduct more experiments. Be open to more trials. Your capacity to try will be linked with your ability to seek help, more help, better help, absolutely anything you need to keep going. By asking for help, you will build the knowledge you need to think forward and achieve the goals you haven't achieved...yet.

Let's put what we learnt in this section into practice. Remember the skill or activity you picked up earlier in "More than one attempt" exercise. Use the template below to ask for help in achieving that goal or completing that activity.

Exercise: I can ask for help

1. I need help with

    _____

    _____

2. The advice I got that will add value to my problem

    _____

    _____

3. My plan to put this advice into action

4. My learnings from putting this advice into practice

5. My next plan of action is

You can download a printable version of "I Can Ask For Help" at:
techtello.com/upgrade-your-mindset/templates/

FACE YOUR CRITICS

How do you react when people around you criticize your work? Do you act defensively or exhibit intellectual humility - recognizing the limits of your knowledge and valuing the insight of someone else?[17] Confident humility, as Adam Grant likes to call it, is having faith in our capability while appreciating that we may not have the right solution or even be addressing the right problem. He says "That gives us enough doubt to reexamine our old knowledge and enough confidence to pursue new insights."[18]

A fixed mindset can disconnect us from reality. Getting defensive when we cannot afford to be defensive: *This can't be right! This is not me! Who are they to tell me how to do things!* Blocking out the harsh truth we need to hear. Echoing our mistaken beliefs in our abilities. Telling us there's nothing more to improve. Making us too self-assured to ask questions. Showing no curiosity in the feedback coming our way and rejecting it even before it has landed. How can we improve when we can't see our own blind spots?

ILLUSION

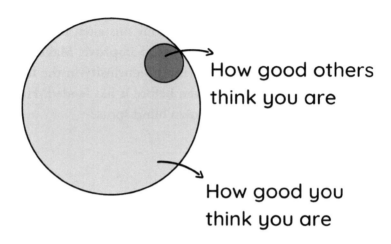

How good others think you are

How good you think you are

NOISE

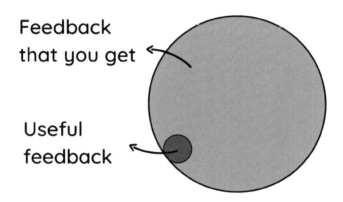

Feedback that you get

Useful feedback

Relentlessly pursuing an idea without making space for criticism can trap us within our own bubble preventing us from getting any better. We need to break out of this bubble, knock down the illusions we have about ourselves and open the door to active criticism. The only way to improve is to actively seek that which we cannot see ourselves or as Ryan Holiday puts it "become a student." In his book, *Ego Is The Enemy*, he writes "You can't learn if you think you already know. You cannot get better if you're convinced you are the best. The art of taking feedback is such a crucial skill in life, particularly harsh and critical feedback. We not only need to take this harsh feedback, but actively solicit it, labor to seek out the negative precisely when our friends and family and brain are telling us that we're doing great."[19]

It can be the other way round too. With critics all around us - family, friends, coworkers, social media, and even the uninvited neighbor, it's easy to get too much feedback. Not knowing how to filter the value from the noise and the good from the bad can make us go downhill. Getting consumed by every remark and every mean comment and treating it as a reflection of our lack of skills, a reminder that we don't have what it takes and others must be right in telling us "we are not good enough." Paralyzed by fear and doubt, we may refuse to put effort into doing the right things, even things that are actually serving us well. The more we refuse to act, the less we achieve. Less we achieve, the more we reaffirm our self-doubts leading to a self-fulfilling prophecy in our fixed mindset.

Solution? Learn to cut through the noise - identify the needle in the haystack, that one piece of wisdom that will help you put a step forward, not ruminating or getting overly consumed by things that aren't useful or don't help you get better. Fight the noise in your head that either rejects every piece of contradicting evidence or inherits every unwarranted conclusion without reflection. Don't operate at the extremes, try to find the balance.

Disconnect the feedback from your identity and see it for what it is - a measure to examine your own shortcomings, identify areas of improvement, develop new strategies to achieve your goals, and a constant reminder that you aren't a finished product, you are still work in progress. There's always more to learn, always another way to do a thing, always a chance to improve, and most importantly, always the mindset to think differently. Thinking that's grounded in treating critiques as investigations or explorations and not conclusions.[20] You may not have a growth mindset…yet. But you can commit to practicing it with every criticism that comes your way.

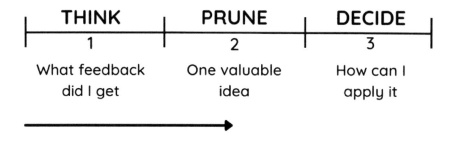

Use this simple framework to act on feedback:

Think about the feedback. Separate words from intent and focus on the key message. What's useful to you - what is it trying to convey? Is it vague? Do you need more information? What data or facts confirm your hypothesis? How are you sure you are not biased in your thinking?

Prune out the advice that doesn't add value and find that one nugget of wisdom that will truly make a difference.

Decide how you plan to put it into action. Deciding to do nothing is also an action as long as it's a conscious decision.

It gets better only with experience. The more you practice the art, the better you get at it. It will take many iterations, you will make many mistakes - both rejecting feedback that was useful as well as implementing things that didn't make so much sense later. Know it's also a part of learning and growth.

Now, let's put the learning from this section into practice. What feedback did you get on the skill or activity we picked up in this chapter? If you haven't done it yet, go ask your critics. Explore all your channels. Get as much feedback as you can. Use the template below to think, prune and decide your next steps.

Exercise: I can act on feedback

1. THINK - What feedback did I get?

   _____

   _____

2. PRUNE - Which part of the feedback is useful to my growth?

   _____

   _____

3. DECIDE - How can I put this feedback into action?

   _____

   _____

You can download a printable version of "I Can Act on Feedback" at: techtello.com/upgrade-your-mindset/templates/

SEE HOW FAR YOU HAVE COME

You may not have yet built the skill or completed the activity we picked up in this chapter. But, do you see that you have made tremendous progress? Do you think you have better tools at your disposal now that can be put to use anytime you want to pick up a new skill or try to solve a problem? We will continue with more strategies and exercises in this book. For now though, it's time to take a pause and look back before investing in more strategies to exercise your growth mindset. Your journey may still be ahead of you, but it's important to reflect on what you have learnt so far.

Examine how far you have come and appreciate all the hard work you have put into exercising your growth mindset. Reflect on both joyful and painful moments as you embrace a new way of thinking. Think about the conflicting emotions you felt in the process. Humour yourself with how something that seemed so complicated earlier, seems simple now. While still a long way to go, congratulate yourself on the progress you have made thus far. Reward yourself with the thing you love to do the most.

Do the exercise below. You can repeat this exercise after every chapter in this book or at regular intervals in your life to continue practicing your growth mindset and identify areas where you can do better.

Exercise: My journey through a growth mindset

Write your journey through a growth mindset. Use these questions to describe your experience:

- Where did you start?
- What strategies did you implement?
- What challenges did you face?
- What worked?
- What didn't work?
- What mistakes did you commit?
- How did you feel?
- What all have you learnt along the way?
- What would you do differently next time?
- Where do you stand now?

_____

_____

_____

_____

_____

_____

_____

_____

You can download a printable version of "My Journey Through a Growth Mindset" at:

techtello.com/upgrade-your-mindset/templates/

"Yet" can be powerful. Not just for you but for everyone around you. Practicing a growth mindset doesn't stop with you. You can create a difference in the lives of so many people you interact with on a daily basis. You can always take a moment to remind them (and in the process yourself) when they say they can't do something or feel like giving up because they just don't know how to do it...yet. You can teach them the strategies you have learned in this chapter and practice them together. They can act as your challenge network, often reminding you and pointing out when you seem to fall back to your old ways of doing things.

In the next chapter, we will learn why expending effort is not the same as lacking talent, how hard work fits into the picture with intellectual ability, and why investing in the right kind of effort matters more than mindlessly going through the motions.

Chapter Summary

- Don't say you can't do something, say you can't do something...yet. Yet is the sound of hope. Show you care about embracing the challenge instead of accepting defeat.
- Keep searching for ways to get better. You might just stumble upon the thing you need. Stop looking and you would have already put an end to your growth.
- Don't rush through change. Achieving anything significant requires more than one attempt. Change your relationship with failure. Use it as a sign to iterate, learn, improve and try just one more time.

- Your identity isn't linked to your ideas. Be open to erase the parts that aren't serving you well. Act with new thinking, a new strategy, a new practice.
- Ask questions, and reach out for help. It does not reflect on your competence. It shows humility and confidence in your abilities to tackle the obstacles that lie in your path.
- Don't just stand around waiting for help to fall in your lap. Actively seek the advice you need, stay honest to your intention, and don't shy away from putting the right assistance into action.
- Act like a sponge. Absorb knowledge and learning from people around you. Criticism does not undermine your intelligence, it's the harsh truth you need to face to see the hidden reality of your situation.

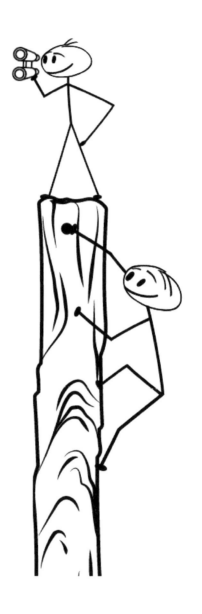

CHAPTER 5

Invest in the Right Kind of Effort

WHEN WE look at other successful people or those who are better than us, we assume they have the talent and we don't. They may have the talent, but you might also be underestimating their effort. They probably tried much harder. They poured in the effort required to develop their talent. They sustained action. They dealt with uncertainty. They learnt from criticism. They pushed outside their boundaries of comfort. They enjoyed the process even though it was painful. They were honest with themselves. Getting good at something not because they were talented or gifted but because they were ready to put up the hours required to grow their talent. Building ability requires curiosity to push ahead, ability to focus, determination, and hard work while seeking challenges and consistently practicing to get better at your game. You may have all the talent in the world, but without determination, effort, and persistence you won't get very far.

TALENT ≠ ACHIEVEMENT

We look at talent and choose to be amazed by its presence - *Wow, she's a natural! He must be really talented! She's gifted! He's a genius!* It's easy to attribute performance and skills to talent without factoring in the labor that goes into their excellence behind the scenes. Feeling thrilled by their outcome while ignoring the input that went into generating that outcome. When we fall for the mystery of the talent and fail to realize that talent, effort, and achievement go together, it makes giving up so easy - *I can never be that! I am not talented enough!* We can fool ourselves into believing we don't have what it takes and quit the attitude to even try.

Angela Duckworth, psychologist, and author says in her book *Grit,* "Without effort, your talent is nothing more than your unmet potential. Without effort, your skill is nothing more than what you could have done but didn't. Talent— how fast we improve in skill—absolutely matters. But effort factors into the calculations twice, not once. Effort builds skill. At the very same time, effort makes skill productive."[1] In other words, stop marveling at the talent and start putting in the effort. It's not your talent, but rather your effort that will decide where you end up.

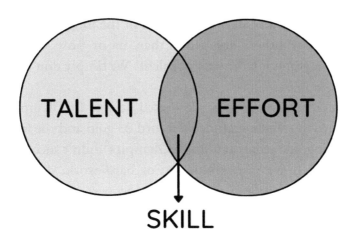

We all want something but are reluctant to put in the effort that goes into actually achieving it. Want to be fit, but not ready to put the effort into working out. Want to be a musician, but not willing to practice notes. Want to be a dancer, but resistant to put in the hours that go into creating a perfect dance sequence. Unwilling to pay the price, we choose comfort in the short term at the cost of building a skill and achieving greatness in the long term. Often left wondering why others are better than us or how they achieved success, we assume it's the lack of talent. We simply don't have what it takes.

Michael Phelps, the most decorated athlete in Olympic history with 28 medals, which included a record 23 gold and the first athlete to win eight gold medals at a single Olympics[2] didn't succeed because of his talent. It was a combination of hard work, determination, intense focus, discipline, and unrelenting perseverance that made him the most decorated Olympian of all time. He was diagnosed with ADHD in sixth grade. "You would think that on the first day I hit the water I just sort of turned into a dolphin and never wanted to leave the pool," he wrote in his book *Beneath the Surface*. "No way. I hated it. We're talking screaming, kicking fit-throwing, goggle-tossing hate."[3] How did he defy all expectations? Regarding the reason for his unmatched success, Phelps said, "I don't want to say it's easy. ... But if you sacrifice, if you're willing to work hard, if you can figure out small little things that make you work, and you have the right people around you -- it's really easy."[4]

J.K. Rowling, the author of the Harry Potter series, started off as a struggling single mother surviving on state benefits. Her novel was rejected by twelve different publishing houses before Bloomsbury accepted it.[5] She was a talented writer, no doubt. But it wasn't talent that made her successful. It was consistent effort. Lots of it. She didn't give up despite facing many rejections. She believed in her work. She worked hard and continued pitching her story with the hope of being accepted someday. Her efforts finally paid off when her book received its first literary award, winning the best Children's book and the British book awards. Her book has been translated into multiple languages and sold more than 500 million copies worldwide. What we now see is the success and not the countless hours she spent writing that novel while barely keeping up with a failed marriage, no job, single parent, and approaching homelessness.

Anyone who has ever made it big knows the blood, sweat, and tears that have gone into their work. Years and years of toiling away and keeping up at it. Some succeeded, and yet many failed despite their efforts. Most of us aren't looking to become great athletes or the biggest names in literature, but we all face challenges in the pursuit of our goals. You do not control the outcome, what you do control is the effort. Are you willing to invest time and energy even if the outcome is not guaranteed? That unwavering relentless drive to show up every day, even when no one is looking, even when it's hard, even when you don't feel like it. Not seeking external validation, but measuring yourself to your own ideal self. Are you doing good work? Are you fulfilling your own standards? Are you seriously putting in the effort?

What if your fixed mindset gets in the way, making you believe that either you have the ability or you expend effort. If you have to work at something, you must not be good at it. Putting in so much effort doesn't seem to make sense when you have already made up your mind that it's not for you. When you expect things to come easily. When learning should happen without practicing. When people should applaud you for your talent and not your effort. You can learn to get past these beliefs. You can learn to admire effort because you now know that ability by itself cannot stand out, it needs effort to become an achievement.

In the rest of the chapter, we will learn how putting in the right kind of effort matters more than mindlessly putting in the hours. If you weren't able to make much progress on the task or activity you picked up in the previous chapter, you can now find out just what you might be missing. After learning new strategies here, combine them with the strategies from the previous chapters and try again. Repeat the exercises and measure your progress.

THINK LONG TERM

Living in a fast-forward, on-demand culture, we all crave instant gratification. We want things quickly. We want them now. Most of the time we improvise and react to events with insufficient information. We don't have patience, time, and energy for more thoughtful long-term solutions. Unwilling to put in the effort, we fall for short-term thinking at the cost of better results in the future. The pursuit of a quick and easy fix to an issue is definitely more alluring than the prudent decision.

As much as we like to believe we are rational in our choices, we give in to our urges which favors short-term payoffs over long-term rewards. Most of us are more likely to accept a $1000 reward now, than a guaranteed reward of $1500 a month from now. Those who smoke cigarettes find it hard to resist the nicotine craving and the pleasure in the moment despite knowing its harmful long-term effects. We may spend a good part of our earnings on buying stuff, more and more stuff - even stuff that we don't need - because the buying experience makes us happy now while not saving enough for the rainy days.

And it isn't one specific area of our life where we fall for the lure of short-term thinking - maximum returns for minimum investment. This is how we think and act. This is how we make decisions in many aspects of our lives. The quickest, easiest way to get to what we want. Solutions that will fix us and make everything alright, overnight. Crash diets that work in two weeks. Six-pack abs in sixty days. Twenty-one secrets to wealth and everlasting success. Hacks to hyper-productivity. We want overnight success with minimal effort and guaranteed outcomes.

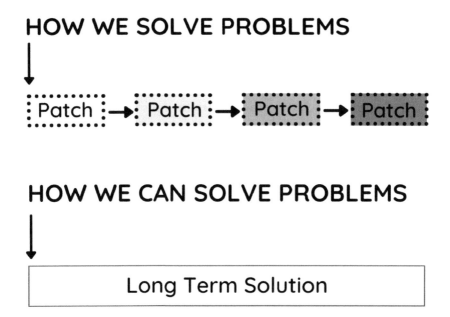

Why do we fall for these quick fixes over and over again when they clearly don't last long? What's our excuse? One simple reason. There's no time to slow down and think. Most of the time we optimize for a small gain in the moment without analyzing the potential impacts of our decision in the future. The speed of achieving something takes priority over its accuracy and validity. We become so obsessed with making the problem go away that we choose the easiest solution that comes to mind while ignoring every other possibility that can be better suited to our problem. As Carl

Honore, author and voice of the slow movement says in his TED talk "We live in a world that's obsessed with speed, with doing everything faster, with cramming more and more into less and less time. Every moment of the day feels like a race against the clock. We used to dial; now we speed dial. We used to read; now we speed read. We used to walk; now we speed walk."[6]

Another reason is the delayed feedback loop. The consequences of our actions aren't readily available. Quick fix provides short-term relief from whatever it is we are facing at the moment. It creates an illusion that the problem is out of the way. But, we fail to realize that these short-term fixes are a series of steps into our long-term failures.

It's not like we lack time and money for more long-term thinking. It's our brain's hardwiring that makes us think and act in the moment. Short-term thinking served us well from an evolutionary standpoint when we were hunter-gatherers foraging for food and trying to avoid being eaten. But, not so much in the world that we live in today. The notification button in the corner of every smartphone app, infinite scroll, and personalized ads are all designed to exploit our short-term focus and feed further into our short-term tendencies. With complex interconnected life, and vast amounts of information to sift through, being able to suppress our short-term instincts is the only way to escape the vicious cycle and invest in more long term-planning that's key to a successful and sustainable future.

Look back and think for a moment about your band-aid solutions. Most likely the band-aid peeled off taking you right back to where you started. And then you threw more time and money at the problem. Another quick fix. Then again, and again and again. Do you see it's a cycle? You get so caught up in making the problem go away that you don't even realize that you are stuck in continually implementing quick fixes. You end up investing more time, energy, and resources into a solution that doesn't even work or worse make your situation unfixable. The price of choosing short-term relief over a long-term fix is usually very high. The debt that you accumulate by ignoring the inevitable needs to be paid over time and is usually very costly.

The only way to avoid the lure of short-term rewards is to show patience and persistence towards a growth-oriented long-term strategy. You need to put in the effort that can be sustained over a long period of time. There's no trick. There's no shortcut. Long-term solutions require hard work. You have to do the work. Solving problems in a hurry rarely works. You need to accept the uncomfortable path. You need to be prepared to face the unknowns and not let them inflict self-doubt, but rather embrace them or as Seth Godin says "when the tough parts come along, the rejection and the slog and the unfair bad breaks, it makes sense to welcome them. Instead of cursing or fearing the down moments, understand that they mean you've chosen reality, not some unsustainable fantasy. It means that you're doing worthwhile, difficult work, not merely amusing yourself."[7] By reviewing each decision with a big picture context, you will have the clarity to attack the source of the problem and avoid the temptation to seek temporary relief by implementing a quick fix in the moment.

This in no way means that quick fixes aren't desirable. Sometimes they are when you need to buy more time to get to the actual solution - a software bug that impacts a large customer base cannot wait for a long-term fix that may take many days and is better off with a quick fix. But a short-term fix shouldn't be treated as a final fix. Effort must be spent in creating the right solution and replacing the temporary fix with a more permanent solution.

Also, everything in life doesn't need an elaborate solution. Some things are better handled as a quick fix. When dealing with complex issues though - trying to build a new skill or solving a problem we have never solved before - long-term thinking is the key to success.

GOAL	SHORT-TERM THINKING	LONG-TERM THINKING
Become healthy	Crash diet	Eat healthy every day
Acquire customers	Spend on marketing	Build a great product
Grow your wealth	Day trading	Invest in stocks for a long duration
Professional success	People-pleasing; engaging in politics	Building skills; consistently doing great work

What about the goals in your own life? What happened when you patched them up - did you learn anything. Did they help you grow? Do you have a solution that works the next time you face something similar?

Let's do this exercise. Think about some of the recent problems you faced and write down the short-term solution you applied and then think of a possible long-term solution to the same problem. It can be any issue you face at work with your boss or colleagues, at home with your spouse or children, or even with a friend. It can also be the issues you face while pursuing a personal goal.

Exercise: Short term vs long term thinking

PROBLEMS FACED	WHAT I DID	WHAT I SHOULD HAVE DONE

You can download a printable version of "Short Term vs Long Term Thinking" at:
techtello.com/upgrade-your-mindset/templates/

RECOMBINE IDEAS

Macintosh was the first computer with beautiful typography - multiple typefaces and proportionally spaced fonts that are now part of every personal computer. It was Steve Jobs' idea to design it all into the Mac. But where did Jobs learn calligraphy when he never even graduated from college? He actually dropped out within the first six months of college. However, he was inspired by how every poster, every label on every drawer, throughout his campus was beautifully hand-calligraphed. So, he decided to drop back in and take calligraphy classes. Luckily Reed college at the time offered the best calligraphy instruction in the country. He learned about serif and sans serif typefaces, about varying the amount of space between different letter combinations, about what makes great typography great. In his finely crafted commencement speech at Stanford in 2005, he describes his experience of learning calligraphy as "It was beautiful, historical, artistically subtle in a way that science can't capture, and I found it fascinating."[8]

While designing the first Macintosh, Steve was able to draw his calligraphy experience from ten years earlier into what seemed like a completely unrelated domain. He could see how it all fits together. He said "None of this had even a hope of any practical application in my life. But 10 years later, when we were designing the first Macintosh computer, it all came back to me. And we designed it all into the Mac. If I had never dropped out, I would have never dropped in on this calligraphy class, and personal computers might not have the wonderful typography that they do. Of course it was impossible to connect the dots looking forward when I was in college. But it was very, very clear looking backward 10 years later." This ability to connect ideas across domains and do what others were unwilling to risk was a major factor in his success with Pixar, NeXT and Apple. He famously said "Technology alone is not enough – it's technology married with liberal arts, married with the humanities, that yields us the results that make our heart sing."[9]

Cross-domain thinking can be extremely powerful to recombine ideas from multiple disciplines - using AI on satellite data to map and predict the progression of wildfires and thereby optimize the response of firefighters. Drones with AI capabilities can also be used to find missing persons in wilderness areas.[10] Do you think these problems can be solved if people in each of these domains refuse to put one foot outside their world?

Not limited to technology, people who have adopted cross-domain thinking have revolutionized industries. Charles

Babbage's invention of computational machines powered by punch cards was inspired by his knowledge of the silk-weaving industry, which used cards with holes to create patterns in the silk fabric. Henry Ford's idea of the car manufacturing assembly line was inspired by Singer sewing machines and meat-packing plants. Claude Shannon combined telephone call-routing technology with his knowledge of boolean algebra to encode and transmit information electronically.

HOW WE THINK

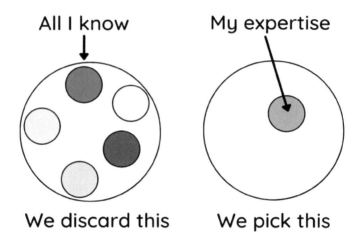

HOW WE SHOULD THINK

What about you? How do you solve problems and fulfill your goals? Do you work within the constraints of your own domain or try to draw knowledge from outside? Do you reason why your specific solution may not work or do you continue digging a deeper hole while sticking to what you know? Solving problems creatively requires making connections between ideas and using everyday life experiences to find solutions between what may seem like disparate problems.

- Learning to deal patiently with a child can be put to use when working with a difficult coworker.
- Knowledge from building blocks that you used as a child can come in handy when you need to design a complex system.
- Mindfulness techniques that you learnt in college can be applied to better your performance in sports.

But why do we fail to leverage cross-domain thinking? It's because we establish rigid boundaries between different aspects of our life. We are reluctant to see how knowledge acquired in one area gels well with the world outside of it. We fail to see patterns, draw inferences, and make connections between ideas that are right inside our own minds. Most of the time, we have enough cognitive tools at our disposal. What we lack is the ability to slow down, think and put them to use - to generate an insight by recombining knowledge in our brain in a whole new way. Drawing knowledge from multiple domains and making connections requires creating mental space for ideas to appear.

Insight = Think outside boundaries + Observe patterns + Make connections

Without the right kind of effort - learning to connect the dots - we may never succeed. David Epstein, who wrote about how generalists triumph in a specialized world, says "Increasing specialization has created a system of parallel trenches in the quest for innovation. Everyone is digging deeper into their own trench and rarely standing up to look in the next trench over, even though the solution to their problem happens to reside there...Modern life requires range, making connections across far-flung domains and ideas...Our greatest strength is the exact opposite of narrow specialization. It is the ability to integrate broadly."[11]

Breaking down these mental barriers can help you invest time in finding solutions as opposed to assuming it's a lack of ability. You don't lack talent. You just weren't looking in the right place. Open the door. Look outside. Learn to recognize situations outside the contexts in which you usually learn about them. Play with your ideas. Challenge yourself. Build the mental muscle to connect an idea in one domain to another domain. With practice, solutions will start to appear where you least expected.

SEEK THE RIGHT LEVEL OF DIFFICULTY

We not only want to lose weight, we need to keep at it. We not only want to start an exercise program, we need to stick with it. We not only want to create strong relationships, we need to establish a bond that lasts. We not only want to do good work once, we need to be able to achieve continuous excellence. Thinking big and setting ourselves goals that at first may seem beyond our reach is the right way to get started. We don't want to settle for too little or too less. But then we get stuck even before we have started - feeling guilty for not doing the things that matter to us and being overwhelmed by the sheer volume and complexity of the task that lies ahead of us. It's too big to attack and keeping at it daily is too much to commit. So, we look for ways to achieve the biggest results in the smallest amount of time; one big dramatic turnaround, a drastic life-altering change.

With our goal to exercise, we start exercising for an hour every day. With our goal to eat healthy, we start eating a bowl of vegetables every day. With our goal to be a runner, we start running 5 miles every day.

Whether we are trying to build a new skill, accomplish a difficult task, or achieve a goal we have set for ourselves, we try to make one giant leap towards improvement while skipping all the steps in between or as Ryan Holiday puts it "We are A-to-Z thinkers, fretting about A, obsessing over Z, yet forgetting all about B through Y."[12] We may achieve some success initially, but it only lasts short. Too much work, too much effort, and just too much commitment. The change isn't simply sustainable and we soon fall back to our old habits. A massive change, or a sudden major improvement never really works. We give up. We stop trying - *Too hard! Can't do it! Not for me!*

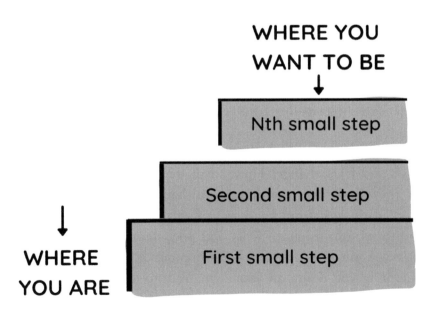

In his book, *One Small Step Can Change Your Life*, Robert Maurer states "Radical change is like charging up a steep hill—you may run out of wind before you reach the crest, or the thought of all the work ahead makes you give up no sooner than you've begun." He suggests another path altogether "one that winds so gently up the hill that you hardly notice the climb. It is pleasant to negotiate and soft to tread. And all it requires is that you place one foot in front of the other."[13]

This strategy of putting one foot in front of the other - taking small steps for continual improvement - is called Kaizen.[14] Lao Tzu, the Chinese philosopher captured the spirit of Kaizen in this famous saying "A journey of a thousand miles begins with a single step" and John Wooden, the legendary basketball coach highlighted the importance of small improvement "When you improve a little each day, eventually big things occur. When you improve conditioning a little each day, eventually you have a big improvement in conditioning. Not tomorrow, not the next day, but eventually a big gain is made. Don't look for the big, quick improvement. Seek the small improvement one day at a time. That's the only way it happens—and when it happens, it lasts."

What's the first small step you can take towards reaching your goal?

Small consistent changes turn off your brain's alarm system that resists and fears change. These small steps may seem trivial at first, but they soon turn into meaningful habits. The small steps create neural pathways through a series of small changes. What was once new turns into a habit. What was once daunting becomes second nature. Soon the new behavior becomes a part of your being, something you desire on your own. You no longer resist change as the new connections in your brain makes you enjoy the experience.

Having mastered the first step, you want to take the second one, then the third, and so on. It's the thrill of the next challenge that makes you want to tune up. As Mihaly Csikszentmihalyi, noted for his work in the study of happiness and creativity, says in his book *Flow*, "One cannot enjoy doing the same thing at the same level for long. We grow either bored or frustrated; and then the desire to enjoy ourselves again pushes us to stretch our skills, or to discover new opportunities for using them."[15]

He adds "Enjoyment appears at the boundary between boredom and anxiety, when the challenges are just balanced with the person's capacity to act."[16] In other words, we seek just the right level of difficulty. Also called Goldilocks Rule, named after the fairy tale Goldilocks and the three bears, the rule states that human beings experience peak motivation when working on tasks that are right on the edge of their current abilities. Neither too easy nor too difficult. Just right.[17] Manageable difficulty rids us of feeling bored with tasks that are easy for us while not getting frustrated when it far exceeds our current abilities.

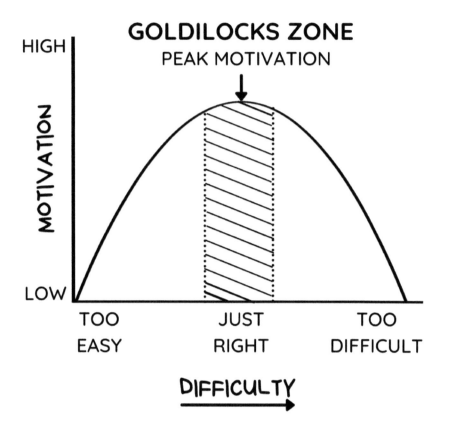

One foot in front of the other requires:

1. Identify a small step and put it into action.
2. Act, revise and repeat step 1 till you seek the second-level challenge.
3. Act, revise and repeat the second-level challenge till you desire the third-level challenge.
4. Repeat this for the third, fourth...nth level challenge.

And just like that, step at a time, your effort will compound into a much bigger change. Goals that seemed too big at first will be now within your reach. There will be no resistance to push aside or delay the task. It will be a part of your identity. It's what you do.

GOAL	ONE STEP AT A TIME
Learn public speaking	1. Practice speaking out loud to an empty room (record, revise, repeat) 2. Practice speaking in front of one person you are comfortable with
To be a writer	1. Write a few sentences every day 2. Write a paragraph every day
Eat healthy	1. Switch a small serving of one meal with a healthy alternative 2. Now do the same with two meals
Be a runner	1. Jog in place (2 mins) 2. Take a few steps forward (1 min), then jog in place (2 mins)

The examples above are not a complete list of steps to reach your goals but should serve as enough guidance to get you started. You can now design your own series of small steps to make progress in your tasks. Remember, small steps that are consistent are the key to achieve long-term goals. Don't fret over missing a day or two. Some situations are beyond your control. Don't use them as an excuse to quit either. Keep coming back to your routine knowing that a large part of your life is still under your control.

TURN INTENT TO ACTION

There is something missing in the steps we discussed in the previous section. Can you identify what is it? Do you think the steps laid out earlier will be sufficient to put your plan to action? What if you forget to take the action or fail to seize the right opportunity? How can you make sure that you don't get derailed by distractions or fall back to old habits? Saying "I will jog in place for 2 mins" or "Write a few sentences every day" is showing good intention. Good intentions don't always translate into accomplishments.

In one experiment, students were asked if they would participate in a study of how people spend their holidays in modern times.[18] Those who agreed had to write an essay while home on vacation, describing in detail how they spent Christmas Eve. The essay was to be written and mailed to the experimenters within forty eight-hours of Christmas Day. Half of the students were requested to write down exactly when and where they would write the essay. The other half were not requested to pick a specific time and place. When students' essays arrived in the mail after Christmas, three-fourths of the students who had specified when and where they plan to take action had written the report in the requested time period, whereas only one-third of the other half managed to do so.

The same behavior is observed with goals that are otherwise difficult to initiate or persist long-term - eating healthy, exercising, reading. In an experiment, researchers in Great Britain took 248 people and divided them into three groups to help them build better exercise behaviors over the course of two weeks.[19] The first group was the control group. They were asked to track how often they exercised over the next two weeks. The second group was the motivation group. They were asked to track their exercise and read material on its benefits. The researchers also explained to this group many of the health benefits exercises could offer them. The third group received everything that the second group received, but were also asked to complete the following statement: "During next week I will partake in at least 20 minutes of vigorous exercise on [day or days] at [time of day] at/or in [place]."

In the first and second groups, 35-38 percent of people exercised at least once per week. But 91 percent of the third group exercised at least once per week - more than double the normal rate. The experiment revealed two major insights:

1. Offering motivation had no meaningful impact on exercise behavior.
2. By simply writing down a plan that specified exactly when and where people intend to engage in these behaviors, they are more likely to follow through.

Peter Gollwitzer, psychologist and researcher on how goals and plans affect cognition, emotion, and behavior calls this desired behavior as creating implementation intentions - making a plan beforehand about when and where you intend to take action. In other words, when situation x arises, I will perform response y.

Implementation intention = I will [DO ACTION] at [TIME] in [LOCATION]

If you haven't been able to follow through on your plans, neither do you lack talent nor do you lack motivation. What you lack is putting your intention to action. All you need is a concrete plan of implementation. Let's explore how you can set implementation intentions for your own goals.

There are two parts to setting implementation intentions:

1. Initiating the action
2. Staying on course

Initiating the action

Unless you create a specific plan detailing when and where you are going to initiate the desired behavior, you will fail to realize multiple opportunities presented during the day when it is possible to make progress on your goals.

Saying "I am going to run tomorrow" without specifying the exact time and location has a much lower chance of follow-through. That's leaving it to chance - hoping you will remember to do the activity, find time to do it, and also feel motivated to do it at the right time. With vague commitments, it's easy to stay busy by doing inconsequential work without ever getting around to doing the specific things you need to succeed. Implementation intention exactly solves this problem. It turns desires into concrete actions "I'm going to run every day for 10 mins at 7 pm outside my apartment."

You no longer need to decide or wait for the inspiration to strike. Should I jog in the morning or the evening? Is it the right time to write? Should I replace a healthy option in this meal or the next one? You can initiate the intended response by simply acting on your plan. Another advantage of implementation intention is that with enough repetition, engaging in goal-directed behavior becomes automatic. You no longer need conscious intent. You automatically act when the situational cue presents itself. Without the hurdles of decision-making and the additional advantage of the right cues in your environment, you can prime yourself to act. But for the execution to be unconscious, forming of the plan has to be conscious.

For example…

I will [DO ACTION] at [TIME] in [LOCATION].

- I will jog Monday to Saturday for ten minutes at 7 a.m. outside my apartment
- I will replace fries with ten sticks of boiled baby carrots at 2 p.m. for lunch in my kitchen
- I will practice public speaking for ten minutes at 8 p.m. right after dinner in my bedroom

Staying on course

Things won't always go according to plan. Unexpected situations might derail you from expected behaviors. Sometimes competing goals may demand your attention. Intended action can be thwarted by attending to attractive distractions. What do you do then? In situations like these, design implementation intentions using the "if-then" version.

Simply put, think about all the obstacles that might interfere with your goal and plan upfront on how to handle them. This way when you do encounter those hurdles preventing you from making progress in your goals, you can use the right strategy to turn them around. You can make the best possible decisions well in advance to keep you on track no matter what comes your way. You can be more flexible to adjust to the unexpected events in your life instead of letting them control your behavior.

For example…

If [THIS HAPPENS], then I will [DO THIS].

- If I cannot jog this Monday morning at 7 a.m. since I have to pick my friend from the airport, then I will do it Monday evening at 6 p.m.
- If I cannot practice public speaking at 8 p.m. on Wednesday since I have to attend a birthday party, then I will practice at 6 a.m. on Wednesday right after I wake up in my bedroom.
- If I am presented with a dessert option when it's my turn to eat healthy, then I will order fruits.

It's time to put this learning into action. Let's do this exercise. Consider a goal you are having trouble implementing. Identify the specific situations in the form of implementation intentions when you can trigger the desired behavior. Now, think about the obstacles that may prevent you from making progress and use an if-then strategy to implement alternative solutions.

Wherever possible, schedule these activities on your calendar or take a printout and stick it where you can see it.

Exercise: Implementation intentions

I will [DO ACTION] at [TIME] in [LOCATION]

I will _____ at _____ in _____

If [THIS HAPPENS], then I will [DO THIS]

If _____ , then I will _____

If _____ , then I will _____

If _____ , then I will _____

If _____ , then I will _____

You can download a printable version of "Implementation Intentions" at:
techtello.com/upgrade-your-mindset/templates/

When you aren't making progress, it's not your talent, but your failure to combine multiple effective strategies and put them to action. No matter what you are trying to accomplish, you are far more likely to succeed when you exercise your growth mindset by learning to put in the right kind of effort. Effort that combines knowledge from multiple domains, visualizes it with long-term thinking, and invests in making small consistent improvements using implementation intentions.

In the next chapter, we will discuss why we are intimidated by others' success, how self-esteem can lead to destructive choices and how self-compassion can save the day.

Chapter Summary

- Ability by itself cannot stand out. It needs effort to become an achievement. You may have all the talent in the world, but without determination, effort, and persistence you won't get very far.
- Using a short-term fix may give you temporary relief from your pain, but usually at a very high cost. Failing to put in the effort that can be sustained over a long period of time

will trap you in a cycle of continually implementing quick fixes.
- Long-term solutions require hard work, but they also signal that you have chosen reality and are doing something worthwhile instead of engaging in a fantasy.
- If you continue to work within the constraints of your domain and refuse to put one foot outside your world, you may never see the patterns or make connections required to solve your problem.
- By putting one foot in front of the other, making small improvements daily and staying consistent in your actions, your efforts will compound into a much bigger change. No drastic life-altering changes, only simple steps one day at a time.
- When seeking a new challenge, put Goldilocks principle to action - human beings experience peak motivation when working on tasks that are right on the edge of their current abilities. Neither too easy nor too difficult. Just right.
- Good intentions don't translate into accomplishment. You need a concrete plan of action using implementation intentions - I will [do action] at [time] in [location].

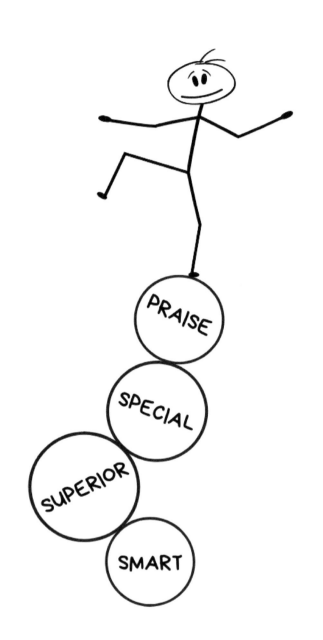

CHAPTER 6

Build Emotional Resilience

IN THE new connected world that we live in today, there's this impulsive need to compare. When comparison is used as a medium for seeking inspiration, learning, and getting better, it can be extremely powerful. However, when it turns into a measure of likability or popularity, it can lead to feelings of inadequacy with severe negative effects on our emotional well-being.

Those who seek external measures of their worth fall on the wrong side of the social comparison on more than one occasion. Instead of becoming the best version of themselves, social comparison can destroy their sense of self-worth. They start seeking external validation and attach it to the number of likes and comments that they get on social media, focus on cultivating an image that does not match who they are in real life, and place more value on other people's approval and their attention.

When all they care about is raising their self-esteem - proving they are smart, special, superior, and better than others - they enter a fixed mindset. In a fixed mindset, their sense of self-worth is tied to success in specific areas of their life. They feel valued when they are successful and not good enough when they fail. When they are successful, they say to themselves: *I am talented! I am superior! It's my intelligence that got me here!* How do they feel when they fail then? *I no longer have what it takes. I am not good enough anymore.* It's as if they are on a roller-coaster ride feeling elated one moment and devastated the next. Worthy one moment and anxious and depressed the next.

This is how it plays out in real life. Let's say you are excited about your new product launch and announce it to the world. A positive comment makes you feel great. The next moment someone criticizes your work and you start doubting everything. All the effort you have put in thus far suddenly looks like a complete waste.

Social media can exacerbate the effect. While scrolling through your social media feed, let's say you read the story of a person who lost their job and is struggling to make ends meet. While you shouldn't rejoice in others' miseries, it does give you a comforting feeling about the security of your own job and how well you are doing in your position. You feel great knowing that you have a wonderful life. As you continue scrolling, you come across an inspirational story of a person who struggled with weight issues and how they worked hard to lose it. Seeing their now perfectly toned body and comparing it to your own challenge with losing weight, you feel ashamed and a complete failure.

Self-esteem is how much we value ourselves and how important we think we are. It's how much we appreciate and like ourselves. It's our overall sense of self-worth or personal value.[1] We establish our sense of self-worth not only from our own judgments but also through the perceived judgments of others. If others think of us positively, we feel good about ourselves. *"Wow! I feel on top of the world. She thinks I am great!"* When others criticize or judge us negatively, we feel bad about ourselves. *"She thinks I am pathetic. I feel small compared to others!"* In other words, our self-esteem is influenced by how we think the outside world sees us.

That makes self-esteem fragile. When our sense of self-worth is tied to seeking external measures of worth - achievement, approval, praise - we fail to notice our own self-destructive patterns of behavior. Mistakes and setbacks turn into personal failures, rather than being a natural consequence of growth. We become so preoccupied with trying to be smart and obsessed with making the right impression on others that we don't even notice when our thinking has clouded our judgment or we have become too self-delusional. We act like the emperor in Hans Christian Anderson's story of The Emperor's New Clothes[2] where the emperor fails to see that he isn't wearing any clothes just because he does not wish to appear foolish.

No doubt, we all need a good dose of self-esteem in our lives. It's what makes us like ourselves and keeps us cheerful. Who wants to disapprove of themselves or feel depressed? The problem occurs when the reward of high self-esteem becomes your only motivator. When you do work only to validate yourself or prove to others how good you are.

- Staying back late at work to show off how hardworking you are.
- Helping a coworker only to show others how helpful you are.
- Doing an activity to establish your intelligence and get that self-esteem boost.

With self-esteem contingent on particular outcomes, will you continue being invested once you stop succeeding? You are most likely to give up once it doesn't give you the validation you need. With a single-minded focus on the outcome and your sense of self-worth tied to that outcome, you fail to learn from the process. Ironically, in your desire to look smart, you fail to adopt behaviors that will make you smart - chasing success leads to ignoring practices that will eventually lead to success, and fear of failure makes you go with easy options even if they don't make you learn.

Your fixed mindset can trap you to adopt behaviors that will raise your self-esteem, prove you are smart and talented, and make you feel good about yourself without effort, determination, hard work, persistence, and struggle that's required to achieve anything significant. There's another problem. A little bit of success with high self-esteem can mess with your mind. It can make you think you are better than others. You are special. You are born smarter than everyone else. When things are going well, all's good. You are successful. You feel worthy. But what happens when things aren't going so well? You feel helpless in the face of substantial challenges and experience a decrease in self-esteem. Flip-flopping between high and low self-esteem, as if you are a victim of your circumstances as opposed to being the creator of the life you want to lead.

Kristin Neff beautifully captures this idea in her book *Self Compassion*. She writes "We grasp onto self-esteem as if it were an inflatable raft that will save us—or at least save and prop up the positive sense of self that we so crave—only to find that the raft has a gaping hole and is rapidly running out of air. The truth is this: sometimes we display good qualities and sometimes bad. Sometimes we act in helpful, productive ways and sometimes in harmful, maladaptive ways. But we are not defined by these qualities or behaviors. We are a verb not a noun, a process rather than a fixed "thing." Our actions change—mercurial beings that we are—according to time, circumstance, mood, setting. We often forget this, however, and continue to flog ourselves into the relentless pursuit of high self-esteem—the elusive holy grail—trying to find a permanent box labeled good in which to stuff ourselves."[3]

She adds "By sacrificing ourselves to the insatiable god of self-esteem, we are trading the ever-unfolding wonder and mystery of our lives for a sterile Polaroid snapshot. Instead of reveling in the richness and complexity of our experience—the joy and the pain, the love and anger, the passion, the triumphs and the tragedies—we try to capture and sum up our lived experience with extremely simplistic evaluations of self-worth. But these judgments, in a very real sense, are just thoughts. And more often than not they aren't even accurate thoughts. The need to see ourselves as superior also makes us emphasize our separation from others rather than our interconnectedness, which in turns leads to feelings of isolation, disconnection, and insecurity."

QUESTIONS WE ASK	QUESTIONS WE CAN ASK
Will this make me look smart	Will this help me learn
Do others approve	Am I improving
What if I fail	What if I don't try
How can I succeed	How good is my process

What if you stopped focussing on your self-esteem and instead do work for the joy it brings? You will embrace opportunities for growth even if it involves risk-taking because you won't fear failure. Setbacks won't lead to experiencing low self-esteem because they signal an opportunity to re-evaluate effort and strategies and not lack of intellectual ability. Progress will be based on how far you've come as opposed to seeking external validation. Instead of comparing yourself to others, you will compare your performance to yourself - Am I improving, staying the same, or getting worse with time? With self-esteem intact, you will focus on the process to achieve mastery. Your success won't be defined by a single outcome. Rather, the process used to achieve that outcome will carry more significance. That's your growth mindset helping you uncover the opportunities you haven't explored yet.

Fixed mindset = Doing work to raise self-esteem; focussed on the outcome

Growth mindset = Doing work to achieve personal mastery; focussed on the process

WHAT'S HOLDING YOU BACK?

How do you feel exactly when someone you know succeeds or performs well in an area of life that's important to you? A colleague who got promoted, a friend who bought a bigger house, or a classmate who's making more money. Are you fascinated by their success or feel diminished by it? Do you feel like a loser, a failure, inferior to them? Does their success indicate you have failed?

Mandy Stadtmiller, author and columnist for New York magazine describes in her famous article how she got rid of her jealousy and other toxic behavior that would make her feel like a loser -

"I started to see clearly the mental prison I had unwittingly trapped myself inside. All this time I felt blinded by everyone else's status. But I was the one who afforded them that status. I saw them as players. But me? No, no, no, no. Energizing questions of personal agency began to rise up. I was starting to call myself on my own bullshit and it felt thrilling, profound.

What if my peers' success wasn't an indictment, but an inspiration?
What if I was exactly like all these people I saw thriving?
What if the main thing holding me back was... me?

I thought about it some more. It's not like these people I felt so jealous of were born with some permission I didn't have. No one gave them some secret license to work their asses off, figure out where opportunities might lie, decide to never be helpless, work their asses off some more, try, fail, try, fail, repeat several more times, and then, eventually, maybe succeed — when success is probably not even the point. The act of creating, of enjoying the journey along the way — that's the point. I realized that if they could do it, so could I."[4]

What's holding you back? Shouldn't others' success be a reason to celebrate?

After all, they are ordinary human beings just like you. If they can succeed, you can too. Their story should serve as a reminder that you have the choice to decide, to pursue what you want, to act in control of your situation, to not believe every thought that enters your mind, to question the path your emotions are guiding you to take and to have utmost conviction in your abilities to turn your desire into a reality. Because only you can determine your story. Instead of feeling threatened and intimidated by the success of others, you can use that knowledge to determine what you have been doing wrong or missing all along. Instead of letting negative feelings make you feel defeated, you can reframe them to feel positive feelings that inspire you to take action.

Amy Morin writes in *13 Things Mentally Strong People Don't Do* "As long as you view the people in your life as competitors, you'll always focus on trying to win. And you can't have healthy relationships with people when you're only thinking about how to beat them, rather than build them up. Spend some time examining those in your life whom you view as your competition. Perhaps you want to be more attractive than your best friend. Or you want to have more money than your brother. Take notice of how viewing these people as your competition really isn't healthy to your relationship. What if, instead, you began to view them as on your team? Including people in your life who possess a variety of skills and talents can actually work to your advantage. If you've got a brother who is good with money, instead of trying to buy just as many expensive toys as he has, why not learn from his financial tips? If you've got a neighbor who is health conscious, why not ask her to share some recipes? Behaving in a humble manner can do wonders for how you feel about yourself, as well as other people."[5]

You can unhook from the trap of the fixed mindset that lowers your self-esteem by comparing and considering other people's success as your failure and turn it around with a growth mindset thinking that considers it an opportunity to finally get the things you want. Don't let your mindset take you down: *I can never be as good as they are! I will never succeed! I don't have what it takes! I feel small compared to them!*

Don't put yourself in the role of a victim by engaging in ruthless self-criticism as it will discourage improvement. Self-criticism can often backfire by increasing your unhappiness levels and making you procrastinate instead of putting in the effort to achieve your goals. Instead feed it with curiosity: *What knowledge do they have that you are lacking? What skills do you need to build? What qualities do you need to adopt? What steps do you need to take to make progress in your goals?* Sit down with these people, talk to them and express genuine interest in their story. Ask more and more open-ended questions. Dig into their answers - how did you learn that, where did you get that information, how was the experience, what else did you try, and what mistakes did you make?

Consciously choosing not to compare is a skill. Competing with none other than yourself requires a mastery mindset. Acknowledging others' success and learning from them takes humility. Surround yourself with successful people. It is a powerful motivator to align your actions with the life you desire.

Let's do this exercise. Look at each of the scenarios below and assume you desire these exact things in your life. Describe the emotion you would feel at first. Don't question it yet. Just write down the first thought that comes to your mind.

Exercise: Competing with self

SCENARIO	HOW DO YOU FEEL
Your team member gets a promotion	
Your sister finds a wonderful partner	

You find your friends beautiful vacation photos online	
Your colleague receives an award	
Your team member is praised by the boss	
Your friend starts earning a much higher salary	
Your spouse acquires a new skill readily (compared to you)	
Your friend shifts into a much bigger house	
Your sister lands herself a public speaking gig	
Your friend's article gets published in a prestigious magazine	

Did you use fixed mindset phrases in any of these scenarios? Now consciously opt-out of it and shift to a growth mindset by reimagining these scenarios with the desire to learn. Repeat this exercise, this time use these situations as opportunities to learn. How can you think like a learner?

SCENARIO	WHAT CAN YOU LEARN
Your team member gets a promotion	
Your sister finds a wonderful partner	
You find your friends beautiful vacation photos online	
Your colleague receives an award	
Your team member is praised by the boss	
Your friend starts earning a much higher salary	
Your spouse acquires a new skill readily (compared to you)	
Your friend shifts into a much bigger house	
Your sister lands herself a public speaking gig	
Your friend's article gets published in a prestigious magazine	

You can download a printable version of "Competing With Self" at:

techtello.com/upgrade-your-mindset/templates/

FAILURE IS PART OF THE PROCESS

How often do you fail? If you are trying to do something worthwhile, then probably all the time. But how do you react to those failures?

- Do they create fear and resistance in your mind?
- Do you worry about how damaging they are to your self-esteem?
- Do you feel anxious about facing criticism?
- Do you try to hide your failures from others?
- Do you give up to avoid failing further?

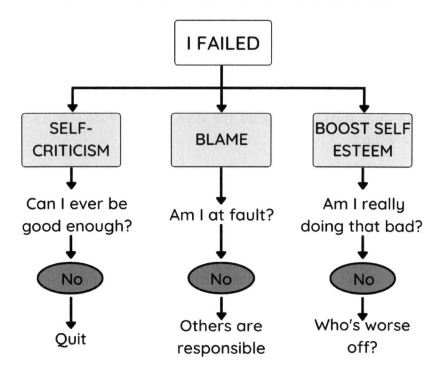

In a fixed mindset, failure is a part of the identity and as a result, it can either make you define who you are: "I failed at this; therefore, I am a failure" or you may adopt the goal of protecting your self-image:

- Continually judging and criticizing yourself which only makes things worse. Feelings of insecurity and inadequacy aren't really helpful. They create a demotivating downward spiral of hopelessness and low self-esteem.

- Attempt to create positive self-esteem by blaming others.[6] Distorting reality takes away your power to act and make corrections.
- Look downwards to people who are doing worse than you are to feel better about yourself. Not a great strategy to learn from your failures.

Got a tough assignment at work that didn't go so well? Your inner voice can tell you *"You are no good!" "You can never get it right. Better quit now!"* Self-criticism will make you feel worse about yourself and stop you from taking action to fix the problem. Why should you try when you know you can't get it right? Now the problem remains and along with it the validation that you really don't have what it takes to solve it, sort of a self-fulfilling prophecy.

If self-criticism is not your thing, you might try to shake off the responsibility by blaming others *"My boss is at fault here. He hates me!" "If only the requirements were clear…"* By avoiding responsibility, you clearly show no intention to identify the root cause of your problem and take steps to set things right. You may also attempt to boost your self-esteem in the moment by looking for people in the organization who aren't doing so well, particularly those who are doing worse off than you are. They can make you feel better about yourself, but with no new strategies to improve, you will be stuck with where you are.

Self-evaluation without engaging in self-criticism is a critical component of self-improvement. Telling yourself you aren't responsible for your failures, aligning your actions with the desire to look good, and taking measures to boost your self-esteem may give you temporary relief from painful feelings in the moment but it does nothing to advance you in the direction of your goals. Without your knowledge, your goal shifts from whatever it is that you wanted to achieve to doing work that will keep your image intact. Emotional depletion shifts your focus from doing work to improving your mood. You are no longer aiming to succeed since you have already accepted defeat. In the words of John Wooden "You can make mistakes, but you aren't a failure until you start blaming others for those mistakes. When you blame others you are trying to excuse yourself. When you make excuses you can't properly evaluate yourself. Without proper self-evaluation, failure is inevitable."[7]

Success and failure are inevitable facts of life. Neither do they define us nor do they determine our worthiness. Absolutely everyone, no matter how perfect they may seem, messes up from time to time. With the right attitude, failure can be a great teacher. Even though it may seem like an interruption from our routine, it's what keeps our foot on the ground. If we don't stumble from time to time, we won't learn how to get up, brush ourselves off and barge forward. As Scott Adams, creator of Dilbert comic strip writes in his book *How To Fail At Almost Everything And Still Win Big*, "Failure is where success likes to hide in plain sight. Everything you want out of life is in that huge, bubbling vat of failure. The trick is to get the good stuff out. If success were easy, everyone would do it. It takes effort. That fact works to your advantage because it keeps lazy people out of the game."[8]

Instead of letting their failures impact their self-esteem, people with a growth mindset accept failures and own them. They understand that short-term failure is the path to long-term success, not separate from it. Continuous learning involves failures before inevitable success. In their desire to do better, they look upwards to people who are doing better than they are to seek inspiration. They strongly lead with what Robert G. Allen, author and most influential investment advisors of all time said "There is no failure. Only feedback." This keeps their self-esteem intact helping them focus on the task at hand by spending their energy in finding solutions as opposed to wasting it in seeking external measures of their worth.

TO SUCCEED FORGET SELF-ESTEEM

How can we learn to better manage our inner voice that either errs on the side of blatant self-criticism or delusional overconfidence on the other extreme? How can we be driven - confident and ambitious while staying real at the same time?

In those moments, when we make a mistake, fail at something, or notice a flaw, engaging in self-criticism - scolding ourselves for being so stupid, judging and criticizing ourselves for our career, relationship, appearance - seems like the most natural response. "What's wrong with me?" "I can't be trusted with anything I say I will do!" "What a stupid thing to say!" "I'm such a loser!" We believe chastising ourselves is the path to be the better version of ourselves. But, it clearly doesn't work. Being highly self-critical or hard on ourselves is not a great motivator. Rather research shows that it leaves us discouraged and depressed.[9]

Think about your younger self. Weren't you free of self-criticism? Dan Millman, author and lecturer in the personal development field once said "Babies don't hold the same tendency toward self-criticism as adults else they might never learn to walk or talk. They don't say "Aarggh! Screwed up again!" They just keep practicing.[10]

Sometimes when we don't engage in self-criticism, we find another way to distort reality - blaming others for everything that isn't going so well for us and refocusing our attention on all the things we do well, boosting our ego with anything that seems satisfying even if it doesn't add value. But why do we need to think positively of ourselves at all times? Why are we so terrified of doing anything that might hurt our self-esteem? After all, new research shows that high self-esteem does not predict better performance or greater success. It does not make you a more effective leader, increase your job performance, be a better partner or choose healthy lifestyle options. High self-esteem is the consequence rather than being the cause of those healthy behaviors.[11]

So, if high self-esteem is not the answer to our problems and it does not lead to growth, then what is?

Research shows that it's possible to be driven while staying real by cultivating self-compassion instead of chasing after high self-esteem. Self-compassion is the ability to face your mistakes and failures with kindness and understanding instead of judging yourself harshly or acting defensive with the goal to protect your ego. It's having the same sense of warmth, empathy, and positive regard for yourself as you would have for another person when they are dealing with a difficult circumstance. Acknowledging that life is sometimes messy and imperfect. After all, to err is human. Kristin Neff, a pioneer in the field of self-compassion research describes it as "Instead of mercilessly judging and criticizing yourself for various inadequacies or shortcomings, self-compassion means you are kind and understanding when confronted with personal failings – after all, who ever said you were supposed to be perfect?"[12]

While self-esteem requires dealing with the ups and downs of positive and negative emotions, self-compassion allows us to embrace our negative thoughts and emotions without judging them as right or wrong. It guides our thinking to act with intention instead of reacting to our feelings by being in better control of our emotions. Many studies show[13] that being compassionate to oneself builds emotional resilience and psychological well-being. People who are self-compassionate:

- Have lower levels of depression and anxiety

- Less likely to ruminate on negative thoughts and emotions or suppress them
- Show increased optimism
- Are able to take personal initiative
- Involved with more positive emotions like kindness, happiness, and connectedness

What about performance - achieving our goals? The biggest misconception about self-compassion is that it can undermine our motivation to push ourselves to do better; being warm and kinder to ourselves makes us lazy. Quite the opposite. Self-compassion is strongly associated with emotional resilience.[14]

Self-compassionate people are more inclined to take responsibility for their actions and strive for the most challenging goals. Research also shows that self-compassion helps people engage in healthy behaviors - intrinsic motivation to exercise, better eating habits, and self-regulation of smoking.[15] With ego out of the picture, they are able to look realistically at their mistakes, identify the things that need to change, and correct their errors to make progress in their goals. The ups and downs turn into useful signals on what works and what doesn't instead of being a reflection of who you are as a person.

Self-compassion provides the intrinsic motivation[16] to do things you say you are going to do, pursue goals based on mastery rather than performance, and lead with less fear of failure. Isn't that what the growth mindset is all about? For a more in-depth understanding of self-compassion and mastering the practice, I suggest you read the book *Self Compassion* by Kristin Neff. She has also provided multiple exercises on her website[17] to put your learning into practice. You must try these exercises to develop a growth mindset through the power of self-compassion.

Now that you have learnt multiple strategies to exercise your growth mindset, it's time for you to take a big bet in your life and put all your learning into practice. In the next and final chapter, we will discuss goals. Why setting the right kind of goals matter, how to set them, and the process to combine your skills and convert them into a plan - a system connected to learning, progress, and growth.

Chapter Summary

- When your sense of self-worth is tied to success in specific areas of your life, you feel valuable when you are successful and not so much when you fail. Emotional ups and downs distract you and drain your mental energy preventing you from focusing on your work.
- When all you care about is raising self-esteem - proving to yourself and others that you are smart and talented, you fail to adopt behaviors and practices that will help you grow. You align your actions with making the right impression on others even if it involves no learning.
- With self-esteem as the goal, mistakes and setbacks turn into permanent failures, rather than being a natural consequence of growth. You stop investing in activities that don't give the validation you need even if they are essential to long-term growth. Short-term achievement and approval takes priority over long-term success.
- Instead of feeling threatened, intimidated, and defeated by others' success, you can reframe your negative feelings with positive ones that inspire you to take action. Feed your mind with curiosity by studying the behaviors, skills, and efforts of successful people.

- Instead of engaging in ruthless self-criticism or passing blame for your failures, accept that continuous learning involves failure before inevitable success.
- Instead of chasing after high self-esteem, cultivate self-compassion - the ability to face your mistakes with kindness and understanding instead of judging yourself harshly or acting defensive with the goal to protect your ego.
- Self-compassion is associated with a growth mindset - pursuing goals based on mastery instead of performance, leading with less fear of failure and being intrinsically motivated to improve.

CHAPTER 7

Craft Your Vision

YOU CAN'T live intentionally without a clear future self in mind. Most of us live a reactive life. Running on autopilot. Letting whatever life throws our way as the guiding force as opposed to deciding and making space for the things we value. Too busy to determine what we want out of life or too lazy to do anything but fantasize about a positive future, we let many opportunities slip by.

When we don't know what we want, it's hard to make the best use of every situation and easy to let distractions eat away into our mental energy and time. Sitting in front of a TV as opposed to using the time to exercise. Engaging in idle gossip with our neighbor instead of taking the time to clean up our closest. Browsing through social media feeds when the same time can be put to use in cooking a healthy meal. When we haven't consciously prioritized exercising, staying organized, or eating healthy as our goal, we not only miss achieving them, we assume the worst *"This is the best we can do!"* We let our future self be an extended version of our limited current self. Why bother setting a goal when we have already made up our mind that we can't achieve it? Our limiting beliefs can kill our desires even before we have given them a chance to turn into reality.

Consciously adopted goals are not only important, they are the only way to lead the life you want. They are your first step into making your dream a reality or as Nikki Giovanni, world-renowned writer, poet, and social commentator puts it "I really don't think life is about the I-could-have-beens. Life is only about the I-tried-to-do. I don't mind the failure, but I can't imagine that I'd forgive myself if I didn't try." Goals by themselves aren't sufficient, but they are the necessary condition to act with intention. They are useful for setting the direction. They define where you want to end up.

And how do you get there? You need sustainable and repeatable systems that give life to your goals. Systems that stick, that work, and that give you useful feedback so that you are not blind to your own progress. In the words of James Clear "Goals are good for planning your progress and systems are good for actually making progress. Goals can provide direction and even push you forward in the short-term, but eventually a well-designed system will always win. Having a system is what matters. Committing to the process is what makes the difference."[1] In other words, your results are all about the systems you follow.

- Your goal is to eat healthy. Your system is organizing your meal plans with healthy options each day.
- Your goal is to become a public speaker. Your system is the practice you follow each week.

- Your goal is to become a swimmer. Your system is the training schedule each week.
- Your goal is to become a leader in your organization. Your system is the work you do each day to build those leadership skills.

Goals = Results you want to achieve

Systems = Process used to achieve those results

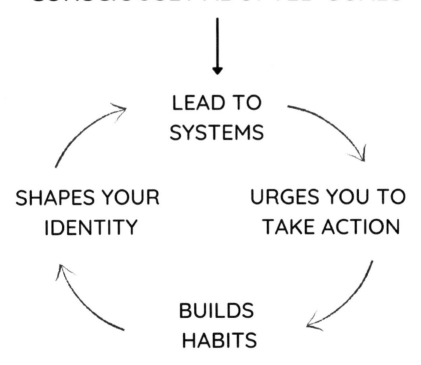

To start, you need to adopt the right goals. Here are some pertinent questions to ask as you get started:

1. How can I make sure the goals I adopt are right for me?
2. What's the right number of goals to have?
3. What if I have conflicting or competing goals?
4. Is it fine to change my goals?

Let's go backward on each of these questions.

Is it fine to change my goals?

Your goals aren't set in stone. Life isn't perfect and so are your plans. Ideally, your goals will require you to go to the drawing board many times. Typically, your top-level goal will remain the same while your medium and low-level goals (more on this later) need continuous iteration as you put your ideas into action, learn from them and incorporate that feedback into your process. A strategy isn't working, you need to formulate a new one. Assumptions you made aren't valid anymore, you need to rewrite your assumptions. A better solution emerges, you need to strike off your old plan to make space for the new one.

What if I have conflicting or competing goals?

Along the way life will present many distractions - new goals will compete and conflict with your existing goals. Your goal to spend time with your family can conflict with your desire to spend time partying with your friends. Your goal to stay healthy can compete with your desire to enjoy food. The problem occurs when we let competing goals and temptations to interfere without adding value.

We diverge from our goals without noticing. In other words, we get distracted and wander into the weeds instead of staying on the path. Instead of doing what we should be doing, we start doing what we could be doing. Result? We lose confidence when we don't get the results we hoped to achieve and give up way too soon.

Zig Ziglar, author and motivational speaker said "Your input determines your outlook. Your outlook determines your output, and your output determines your future." In other words, once you decide what you want, you have to pay attention to everything you let into your life - the information you consume, people you surround yourself with, and the way you design your environment. Eliminate everything that conflicts with your goals. Consciously shoot down goals that demand your attention and stand in the way of achieving goals that matter. Create an environment that matches your goals by filling it with productive cues and eliminating unproductive ones. We respond strongly to the cues that surround us.[2] For example, if you want to eat healthy, organize your household with healthy options instead of letting junk food interfere with your desire to eat healthy. If you want to do yoga every morning, leave your yoga mat every night in the middle of the living room.

What's the right number of goals to have?

Many goal-setting advice will direct you to focus on one big goal at a time. However, the idea that every waking moment in our lives should be guided by one top-level goal isn't desirable in my own life. Does having a career mean I cannot be a great mother to my daughter? These goals aren't conflicting. Both are necessary for the life I want to build for myself and my family. Are they easy? Absolutely not. Ideally speaking, all our goals compete with each other since time spent working on one goal is usually time not spent working on other goals. This in no way means that I need to give up on my desire to be a great mother while also wanting to do well in my work. It does take a little bit of planning, but both are possible.

If you ask me, there's no right and wrong answer for the number of goals you should choose for yourself. It all depends on what you want and what's right for you. I definitely don't advise having too many goals either. They take away your ability to focus on what's truly important to you. One top-level goal for each important area of your life should do the trick. For example, I personally keep one goal each for family, work, and personal development.

How can I make sure the goals I adopt are right for me?

Scott Adams, the creator of the Dilbert comic strip, writes in his book *How to Fail at Almost Everything and Still Win Big* "Successful people don't wish for success; they decide to pursue it. And to pursue it effectively, they need a system. Success always has a price, but the reality is that the price is negotiable. If you pick the right system, the price will be a lot nearer what you're willing to pay."[3] To adopt the right goals you need the right system. The next section on goal setting covers this topic in detail. I will guide you through the step-by-step process for setting your goals.

With the right mindset, you don't daydream about fulfilling your goals. You actually create systems to achieve them. Right system urges you to take action. Consistent action leads to positive habits that reinforce the identity of the person you wish to become.

GOAL SETTING

Some people may already know what they want. All they need is a little bit of time and some degree of focus to organize their thoughts and prioritize what truly matters to them. Others probably need more time to contemplate and determine what they'd like to accomplish. Either way, remember it's a process. Getting to a state where the goal feels just right will require many iterations. You may not get it right the first time. That's fine. Start with something. Learn from the process. Revise your goals as you go forward.

There are three steps to goal-setting:

1. Connect to your life philosophy
2. Think about your motivation
3. Make them about your identity

Let's discuss each step in detail.

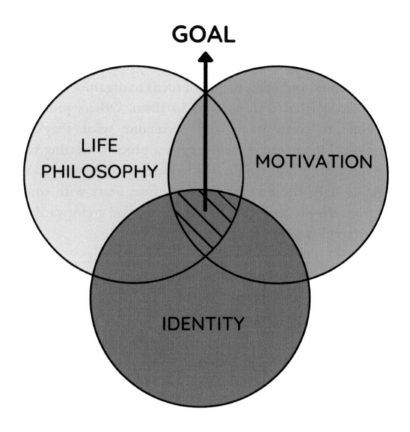

Step 1: Connect to your life philosophy

Your life philosophy determines who you are and what you stand for. A lens that guides all your thoughts, words, and actions. Something that gives you guidelines and boundaries to keep you on track. Your life philosophy gives direction to your top-level goal that acts as a compass and gives meaning to all the goals below it. It helps you stay connected even during your most difficult times and setbacks. When dealing with life challenges, it guides you to stay resilient, to stay on course, to fight back failures, and to devise new strategies for moving forward and continue being effective.

Pete Carroll, head coach of the Seattle Seahawks, puts it this way "The power of knowing your personal philosophy comes from knowing yourself. When you are clear on what's important to you and what you stand for, you are equipped to handle life. This "knowing" gives you strength and conviction to deal with life's challenges. And your philosophy allows you to believe and trust in yourself."[4]

To determine your top-level goal, ask yourself these questions:

1. What changes you'd like to make (What's important to you)?
2. Why do you want to make them (more on this in step 2)?
3. What costs are you willing to pay to make this happen?

Writing down your top-level will take work. It's an intense process of self-reflection where you actively weigh the things you need to give up to be able to make space for the things you value. It's being clear about the trade-offs - achieving this goal will always come at the cost of not achieving something else. You must be willing to accept the sacrifices required to achieve your goal. You have to be ready to endure the process that comes before any successful outcome.

Who doesn't want to be happier, healthy, and wealthy? Everybody wants to achieve these goals. But you don't want to end up signing for a fantasy. Doing this exercise and knowing the costs will help you stay real about your goals. Mark Manson, author and blogger writes "Who you are is defined by the values you are willing to struggle for. You can't have a pain-free life. It can't all be roses and unicorns. And ultimately that's the hard question that matters. Pleasure is an easy question. And pretty much all of us have similar answers. The more interesting question is the pain. What is the pain that you want to sustain?"[5]

- If your top-level goal is to be a runner, are you willing to face the aches, pains, muscle soreness, and common injuries that affect runners?
- If your top-level goal is to be healthy, are you willing to organize your life planning the kinds of food you need to eat, exercises you have to do, and temptations you have to get rid of?
- If your top-level goal is to be a great parent, are you willing to spend quality time with your children without the distractions of work and digital life?

It's easy to sit around and want all the good things in life, but the only people who succeed are the ones who are willing to make the trade-offs and accept the costs that come with building the life they want. Remember, if anything in your life is going to change, it would have to begin with you. If you didn't change, nothing else would change. Don't let your fixed mindset tell you that you don't have the talent and abilities required to make this change. Don't let it create fear of failure. Don't let it drive you away from visualizing your future and setting life goals to align your actions with the life you want to build for yourself.

Step 2: Think about your motivation

While setting goals in the previous step, one of the questions was "Why do you want to make this change?"

Think about it - what's your motivation for making this change? Self-Determination Theory (SDT)[6] of human motivation developed by psychologists Edward Deci and Richard Ryan compares autonomous motivation (intrinsic motivation) and controlled motivation (extrinsic motivation). They write "Autonomous motivation involves behaving with a full sense of volition and choice, whereas controlled motivation involves behaving with the experience of pressure and demand toward specific outcomes that comes from forces perceived to be external to the self."

Is your desire to lose weight and get into a specific body size driven by external motivation like meeting society's standards? Or is it driven by your own internal motivation where eating healthy or exercising regularly makes you feel better? Do you want to get into a leadership position to boost your self-esteem and prove to others how capable you are? Or are you motivated by the desire to create an impact and drive business growth in your organization?

Psychologist Ken Sheldon's work shows that enjoyment and importance are two main components of autonomously motivated goals.[7] When we work on goals to meet other people's demands or out of necessity, we rarely feel the satisfaction that comes with achieving goals. It's the accomplishment of goals caused by internal motivations such as interests, desires, values, and identities that fulfill us.

When you are intrinsically motivated, your own internal reward system in the form of positive emotions acts as a powerful force to pursue the task. You repeat behaviors that are fulfilling because the activity itself seems pleasurable. It's a process that you enjoy repeating every single day. The joy of acting inline with your values inspires you to keep going even when you face setbacks and challenges. When your top-level goal aligns with what you intrinsically desire, you crave the journey without obsessing about the outcome. Now ask yourself, is the top-level goal you identified earlier driven by internal or external motivators?

Step 3: Make them about your identity

We discussed in Chapter 2 that anything you try to do which is not in alignment with your identity won't last long. Conflict with the self will be too strong to implement any everlasting change. Instead of setting outcome-based goals, you need to set identity-based goals. In other words, align your top-level goal with the person you wish to become. Once your goal becomes a part of your identity, it's easier to align your actions with it. Your goal isn't to run ten miles every day, it's to become a runner. Your goal isn't to lose ten pounds, it's to become healthy. Your goal isn't to speak at TEDx, it's to become a public speaker. Your goal isn't to attend your daughter's school program, it's to be involved in her life and connect with her so that she can approach you when she needs you. Now think about your top-level goal from step 1 and reframe it by shifting from outcome-based goals to identity-based goals.

At this stage, it's important to know that setting a top-level goal is just the beginning. It's what gives way to your medium and short-term goals - the specific things you need to do to act like the person you wish to become. Your top-level goal will continue to be a wish until you take specific steps to turn it into a reality. We will cover medium and short-term goals in the subsequent sections.

In a study conducted by Dr. Gail Matthews, a psychology professor at the Dominican University in California, they found that those who wrote their goals accomplished significantly more than those who did not write their goals.[8] Brian Tracy, author and motivational speaker has echoed the idea. He writes "People with clear, written goals, accomplish far more in a shorter period of time than people without them could ever imagine."[9]

Let's do this exercise. Write down your top-level goal. Don't rush through the exercise, writing it down will take work. Revisit and revise as you get closer to discovering your values. I suggest writing down your top-level goal in each of these three areas - your work, family, and personal growth. Thinking only about one while ignoring others can make you neglect them or they can interfere with each other leaving you confused and frustrated. Clarifying what you value most in each of these areas will help you plan how to spend your time. Remember to think about these goals using your values, aligning them with what you intrinsically desire, and connecting them with the identity you wish to build for yourself.

Exercise: Top level goal setting

1. What's my top-level goal in my area of work?

   _____

   _____

2. Why is this work goal important to me?

   _____

   _____

3. What costs am I willing to pay to fulfill this work goal?

   _____

   _____

4. What's my top-level goal for my family?

_____

_____

5. Why is this family goal important to me?

_____

_____

6. What costs am I willing to pay to fulfill this goal for my family?

_____

_____

7. What's my top-level goal for my personal growth?

_____

_____

8. Why is this personal growth goal important to me?

_____

_____

9. What costs am I willing to pay to fulfill this personal growth goal?

_____

_____

You can download a printable version of "Top Level Goal Setting" at: techtello.com/upgrade-your-mindset/templates/

These top-level goals may look big and scary. How do you go from here to actually making things happen? In the remaining sections, we will design a solid system for achieving these goals.

FEAR SETTING

Fear is a very real feeling and left unattended it can wreak havoc in our lives. Fear can make us imagine the worst possible scenarios that are highly unlikely and use them as an excuse for inaction. Fear can make us feel nervous about the change and put things off with the fear of the unknown. Fear can make us live in optimistic denial and let rationalization interfere with our ability to think clearly - sort of an illusion where we assume that things will somehow magically get better.

Since fear impacts your emotions which in turn impacts your ability to make decisions, it can interfere with your goals by amplifying the risk of acting on your goals. Without getting your fears in check, you cannot push forward with full momentum towards your goals. In order to get a good grip on your fears, you need to sit down with your fears and define them.[10] This one comes from Tim Ferriss, author and lifestyle guru. Let me explain how this fits into the world of goals through Tim's own story.

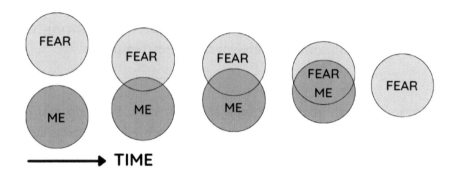

Tim Ferriss tells of a time when he was making a lot of money, but at the same time he was completely miserable. He had no time and was working himself to death. He set goals and made resolutions to change direction, but nothing happened. He was insecure and scared - what would happen to his business if he stopped working 15-hour days? He wanted to take a trip, make his business self-sustaining and break from his workaholic schedule. He let his shame, anger and embarrassment prevent him from taking the trip for six months. Then one day he hit upon an idea - deciding the worst thing that could happen as a result of this trip, facing his biggest nightmare.

He writes "In my undying quest to make myself miserable, I accidentally began to backpedal. As soon as I cut through the vague unease and ambiguous anxiety by defining my nightmare, the worst-case scenario, I wasn't as worried about taking a trip. Suddenly, I started thinking of simple steps I could take to salvage my remaining resources and get back on track if all hell struck at once. I realized that on a scale of 1–10, 1 being nothing and 10 being permanently life-changing, my so-called worst-case scenario might have a temporary impact of 3 or 4. On the other hand, if I realized my best-case scenario, or even a probable-case scenario, it would easily have a permanent 9 or 10 positive life-changing effect."

Once he defined his nightmare, his worst-case scenario, he realized that he was worried about an unlikely and temporary one-in-a-million disaster nightmare while letting go of a more probable and permanent positive life-changing effect. The exercise ended with a significant realization - there was practically no risk, only huge life-changing upside potential. He bought a one-way ticket to Europe. As he traveled, his business did so much better that it financed his travel around the world for 15 months.

Defining fear = Conquering fear

Seneca, the Roman Stoic philosopher said "We suffer more often in imagination than in reality." Tim's example also shows that we exaggerate the fear in our minds and it only gets worse unless we take time to face our worst fears. He writes "To do or not to do? To try or not to try? Most people will vote no, whether they consider themselves brave or not. Uncertainty and the prospect of failure can be very scary noises in the shadows. Most people will choose unhappiness over uncertainty." What's the antidote to fear? Laying out a plan to deal with your fears will make it more likely that you follow through on the changes you want to make.

The fear setting template[11] provided by Tim Ferriss is just what you need before you dive into your goals and decide on the steps to achieve them. Facing your fears upfront will help you focus your time and energy into putting your ideas into action instead of letting them mess up with your plans.

Let's do this exercise. Use this fear-setting template provided by Tim Ferriss (modified for clarity) to face your fears. In the first step, write down everything you dread might happen if you decide to take an action. Then, for each fear, write down the specific actions you can take to prevent the situation from happening or the actions you can take to get back on track if you do end up facing your worst nightmares. In the second step, list down all the positive things that might happen if you take this action. As the final step, think about the costs you need to incur if you don't act now.

Exercise: Fear setting

STEP 1 - WHAT IF I?

DEFINE	PREVENT	REPAIR
What's the worst that could happen if you take action • Be specific • Define your worst nightmares • Rate 1-10 for impact	What specific actions could you take to reduce the likelihood of this situation happening • Be specific • Consider both big and small actions	If this situation does happen, what would you need to do to get back to where you are or get back on the right track

STEP 2 - WHAT MIGHT BE THE BENEFITS OF AN ATTEMPT OR PARTIAL SUCCESS?

BENEFITS (RATE 1-10 FOR IMPACT)

STEP 3 - COST OF INACTION
(EMOTIONALLY, PHYSICALLY, FINANCIALLY, ETC.)

6 MONTHS	1 YEAR	3 YEARS

You can download a printable version of "Fear Setting" at:
techtello.com/upgrade-your-mindset/templates/

CLIMBING THE MOUNTAIN

Imagine two people standing at the foot of the mountain with the same goal of reaching the top. One attacks the goal with a solid system designing every step to the top, using specific checkpoints to measure their progress, feedback loops to implement continuous improvements, and carefully designed experiments to handle failures and setbacks. The other person jumps to action right away without a proper strategy, never stops to measure their progress, rarely uses feedback to course-correct, and applies quick fixes to deal with failures and setbacks. Who do you think has a higher likelihood of reaching the top?

In all measures of goal success, a well-designed system will beat a poorly designed one all the time. As Pablo Picasso, one of the greatest and most influential artists of the 20th century once said, "Our goals can only be reached through a vehicle of a plan, in which we must fervently believe, and upon which we must vigorously act. There is no other route to success." How can you climb your own mountain to the top?

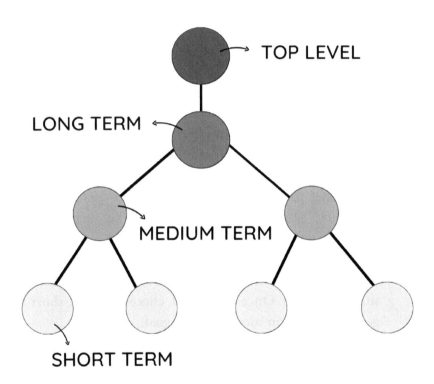

Imagine your goals in a goal hierarchy[12] with your top-level goal sitting at the top of the hierarchy followed by multiple levels of long-term goals followed by multiple levels of medium-term goals followed by multiple levels of short-term goals. Your short-term goals are the specific actions you need to take in 1-2 weeks that add up to fulfill your medium-term goals that might take 3-6 months to accomplish which further roll into your long-term goals which may take a year to complete.

Instead of creating three or five-year plans which are too complicated to maintain and track, I recommend setting yearly goals - specific things you want to achieve that year. This is the way it works:

1. Choose a sub-goal of your top-level goal that you want to accomplish in the next one year. This is your long-term goal (1-year goal).
2. Select a medium-term goal that you can accomplish in the next 3-6 months. It's ideally a big part of your long-term goal.
3. Find a short-term goal that you can accomplish in 1-2 weeks. Remember implementation intentions discussed in Chapter 5. Your short-term goal should be set using an implementation intention so that you know when and where you plan to take action.
4. Now get down to work and focus on completing this short-term goal. Once completed, choose the next short-term goal to get to your medium-term goal.
5. Once a medium-term goal is accomplished, choose a new medium-term goal to get to your long-term goal (1-year goal).
6. Once your long-term goal is completed, choose another long-term goal and repeat these steps.

Here's an example:

Top-Level Goal	Stay healthy
Long-Term Goal (1 year)	Run thrice per week for thirty minutes
1st Medium-Term Goal (3 months)	Run twice per week for fifteen minutes
1st Short-Term Goal (2 weeks)	Jog for five minutes [Monday and Wednesday at 6:30 A.M outside my apartment]
2nd Short-Term Goal (2 weeks)	Run for five minutes [Monday and Wednesday at 6:30 A.M outside my apartment]
3rd Short-Term Goal (2 weeks)	Jog for five minutes and then run for five minutes [Monday and Wednesday at 6:30 A.M outside my apartment]
4th Short-term Goal (2 weeks)	Run for ten minutes [Monday and Wednesday at 6:30 A.M outside my apartment]
5th Short-Term Goal (2 weeks)	Jog for five minutes and then run for ten minutes [Monday and Wednesday at 6:30 A.M outside my apartment]
6th Short-Term Goal (2 weeks)	Run for fifteen minutes

	[Monday and Wednesday at 6:30 A.M outside my apartment]

In the example above, 1st to 6th short-term goals add up to fulfill the 1st medium-term goal. Once accomplished, you can set a 2nd medium-term goal and repeat the process. Design 2nd...nth medium-term goals such that each goal takes you closer to where you want to be, your long-term 1-year goal.

Michelangelo Buonarroti, a Renaissance artist once said "The greater danger for most of us is not that our aim is too high and we miss it, but that it is too low and we hit it." Edwin Locke and Gary Latham, two eminent organizational psychologists have found that goals that detail out exactly what needs to be accomplished (specific), and that set the bar for achievement high (challenging) result in far superior performance than goals that are vague or that set the bar too low. When setting these goals, don't aim too low. Don't aim to do your best. Don't settle for too little with a fear of failure. Don't let your fixed mindset set the limits on what you can accomplish. Set specific and challenging goals.[13]

While thinking about your goal hierarchy, you may struggle to settle in for one long-term goal or face a problem identifying short-term goals that add up to your long-term goals. It's not uncommon to find it hard to select one long-term goal when so many other goals compete for your attention or to break down a long-term goal into a series of medium and short-term goals that fit together. Well, not anymore. I am going to help you create a system for selecting your long-term and short-term goals.

How do I choose a long-term goal?

To identify a long term-goal (1-year goal), follow this process. For each top-level goal:

1. Write down 10-15 long-term goals that align with your top-level goal. It's fine if you can't think of 10-15 goals. Write down as many as you can. Idea is to think deeply about every action that can contribute to your top-level goal.
2. Revisit the list created above and look for patterns and common themes amongst these goals. Identify the goals that can be combined together into one main goal.
3. To each of these goals, assign a score of 1-10 on a scale of importance with 1 being the least important and 10 being the most important, then again a score of 1-10 on a scale of interest with 1 being the least interesting and 10 being the most interesting.
4. Pick the goal with the highest score on the importance and interest scale as your first long-term goal. It's quite unlikely that multiple goals will have the same importance and interest score. If they do, in all likelihood they are part of the same goal. Rethink how they can be combined into one long-term goal.

Here's an example:

Top-level goal for family: Build a strong bond with people close to me

Possible Long-Term Goals (1 Year)
Take one week vacation every three months
Spend two hours daily with my children without digital distractions
Take kids out for their basketball / football / swimming practice sessions
Do laundry three times every week (share responsibilities with my spouse)
Eat dinner with my family five days every week
Attend my kids' school programs
Spend an evening every weekend with my spouse doing things we both enjoy
Visit my parents every three months
Attend festivals and celebrations with people close to me
Prepare breakfast three times per week

How do I identify my short-term goals?

To identify and connect short-term goals that fit into your long-term goal, use a Simpleology system called backward planning devised by Mark Joyner.[14] Here's how it works:

1. Start with a clear end-state - a clearly defined goal with a clearly defined outcome. This is your long-term goal identified in the previous step. You should be able to visualize what it looks like when you have achieved the outcome. For example, let's say your long-term goal (1 year) is publishing an online course. Visualize what achieving this state would look like.
2. Then ask yourself, "Right before this end-state is achieved, what is the very last thing I will do?" In the example above, the very last step you will do is press the publish button and make the course available to everyone.
3. Then figure out what you'll need to do just before that step. In the example above, you will review your course to make sure all assets are in place before pressing the publish button.
4. Then think about the step before that, and so on, until you get to the first step. This first step is your first short-term goal. In this example, the first step might be to brainstorm ideas for your online course. As you follow this exercise, you will get all the steps linked to achieving your goal.

Setting goals and achieving them doesn't look all that difficult once you follow a process. Climbing the top of the mountain won't be scary. No giant leaps. Only small forward steps in the direction of your goals. As Tom Hiddleston, an actor once said "You never know what's around the corner. It could be everything. Or it could be nothing. You keep putting one foot in front of the other, and then one day you look back and you've climbed a mountain."

Put this learning into practice by creating your own goal hierarchy using the template below. Do this exercise for every top-level goal.

Exercise: Goal hierarchy

LONG TERM GOAL (1 YEAR)	MEDIUM TERM GOALS (3-6 MONTHS)	SHORT TERM GOALS (1-2 WEEKS)
	1.	1.
		2.
		3.
		4.
	2.	1.
		2.
		3.
		4.

You can download a printable version of "Goal Hierarchy" at:
techtello.com/upgrade-your-mindset/templates/

BRIDGING THE GAP

Why do so many people fail to do what they know is right? They don't have the skills required to achieve their goals and get impatient with the process of building new skills. Building a new skill takes longer than expected. Building a new skill is hard work. Learning a new skill requires extreme commitment. People fail to build the skills because they do not give it the dedicated and focused attention that it deserves. They want instant gratification and feel overwhelmed and discouraged with the slow progress. In those moments of struggle - when their effort fails to show results, when they make a mistake or when they find it hard to push forward, their fixed mindset can get in the way: *"Are my goals even achievable?" "What if I never achieve them?" "Why should I try if I am never going to succeed?" "I don't have what it takes to build this skill."*

They fail to realize that they don't lack the ability to build the skill, they need a new strategy to make progress. They aren't failing because they are not good enough, they are failing because failure is a natural part of growth. Instead of questioning whether they can achieve a goal or not, they should question if they are working on the right skill. Every new skill is an investment. Is the investment worth it? Is it aligned with their goals? What would get better once they acquire this skill?

Most of the time it's not the goal, it's your process and attitude to achieve that goal that needs to change. You can develop lofty goals, but you cannot fulfill them without developing a growth mindset. What stands in the way of where you are now to where you want to be - skills, obstacles, and challenges? The only way to overcome these obstacles and build any new skills is by developing a growth mindset first. Because once you have a growth mindset, you are willing to experiment, you want to try, you don't give up easily, you re-evaluate your strategies, you consider failure as learning opportunities, you are patient with your progress and you are ready to ask for help.

- Don't question your ability, question your process.
- Don't question failure, question your learning.
- Don't try to prove yourself, try to improve yourself.
- Don't focus on the results, focus on the journey.

Your growth mindset not only helps you adopt the right goals for yourself, it helps you build the skills needed to master those goals. It helps you spend less time lamenting and more time putting your ideas to action. It helps you climb out of the hole when you face a setback. It helps you develop the resilience required to be flexible in an uncertain world. It helps you deal with a challenge by building the skills required to deal effectively with that challenge. Only your growth mindset can bridge the gap between where you are now to where you want to be.

The following quote from Lao Tzu captures the idea well:

> Watch your thoughts, they become your words.
> Watch your words, they become your actions.
> Watch your actions, they become your habits.
> Watch your habits, they become your character.
> Watch your character, it becomes your destiny.

—LAO TZU

Chapter Summary

- Consciously adopted goals set the direction on the life you want to lead. Instead of letting your limiting beliefs set the limit on what you can achieve, exercise your growth mindset to set challenging goals.
- Goals by themselves aren't sufficient, you need solid systems to give life to your goals. Your process will determine the progress you make on things that matter to you.
- Life isn't static and so are goals. As new goals compete for your attention and temptations interfere with your ability to focus, don't get distracted. Shoot down goals that aren't helpful and organize your environment with productive cues to enable goal fulfillment.
- The idea that one top-level goal should guide all our actions is unrealistic. Defining one top-level goal each for your work, family and personal growth will keep things in balance.
- To adopt the right goals for yourself, connect to your life philosophy to identify the changes you would like to make, ensure it's intrinsically motivating, and align it with the person you wish to become.
- Use the fear-setting exercise by Tim Ferriss to get rid of your unwanted fears before putting your goals into action. This will ensure you don't put off things with the fear of the unknown or let rationalization interfere with your ability to think clearly.
- Create your own goal hierarchy by choosing a long-term goal followed by medium and short-term goals to take consistent small steps in the direction of your goals.

- Be patient with the process of building new skills. Use your growth mindset to engage with the challenge and confront obstacles to build the skills you desire. Only your skills can bridge the gap between where you are now to where you want to be.

MINDSET TRACKER

UNLESS YOU commit to a lifelong journey, you won't deepen your understanding of the growth mindset and use it productively in your life. You don't want to read the book, feel good about the exercises and then forget about them. It will be like any other book that helped you for a while and then stopped being useful the moment you put it down.

Just like your calendar helps you schedule your priorities and routines help you ease out the difficult tasks, this tracker will serve as a daily reminder to practice your growth mindset. You won't need to spend more than a few minutes to update it. It will be worth your time as you will see the benefits of this habit compound over time.[1]

Leo Babauta, creator of Zen Habits states "If you do something small repeatedly, the benefits accrue greatly over time. It's obvious, but not everyone puts it into practice. Adding little amounts over time makes a huge difference. And the benefits aren't just the small amounts added up — there's interest accrued as well."[2] Small investments of your time can have huge dividends in the future.

Start with noting down daily progress and as you become familiar with the process, convert it into weekly tracking. You can either use a calendar at home or take a printout of this tracker available online and stick it where you can see it.

To use this tracker,

- Block a small interval, 10-15 mins of your time each day.
- Now, recall all the events from the day and try to take a mental note of the instances when you exercised your growth mindset vs when it was your fixed mindset that came to the forefront. If writing it down helps you do this exercise better, take quick notes as you recollect various events.
- Assign a score of 1-10 to your fixed mindset and growth mindset - 1 being the least likely and 10 being the most likely. This score is based on how you reacted to various events during the day and which mindset was least likely or more likely to be used.
- Once you have your scores, put them on the tracker as F [Your Score] / G [Your Score] where F stands for the fixed mindset and G for the growth mindset. Do this daily and see how your mindset is playing out each day. Are you noticing more growth mindset triggers or fixed mindset triggers? Is there a pattern you can observe in the events that trigger your fixed mindset?
- Consolidate data from the daily tracker to the weekly tracker and calculate totals over the month to keep a visual record of how you are progressing.

After completing all the exercises in this book, continue using the tracker to see how you are doing. By keeping a record of your scores, you will include moments of self reflection[3] into your daily schedule and that will help you separate effective from ineffective strategies.

This quote from Iyanla Vanzant sums it up beautifully "Until you take the journey of self-reflection, it is almost impossible to grow or learn in life."

You can download a printable version of "Mindset Tracker" at: techtello.com/upgrade-your-mindset/templates/

BONUS

Promoting Growth Mindset in Kids

IF YOU are a parent, you will not only benefit from developing a growth mindset yourself, but also from promoting this mindset in your kids.

Research has shown that mindset plays a critical role in children's health and overall development.[1] Growth mindset leads to higher achievement in students since they take on challenges and learn from them, thereby increasing their abilities and achievement. They understand that effort makes them stronger and are willing to put in extra time and effort.[2] Growth mindset also leads to better math grades.[3]

While the ideas in this book can be applied to just about everyone, some specific strategies and interventions can be extremely powerful to develop a growth mindset in kids. I have put together a bonus chapter on developing a growth mindset in kids backed by research with plenty of resources to help your child put their learning into practice.

You can download this chapter at:
techtello.com/upgrade-your-mindset/promoting-growth-mindset-in-kids/

I hope we can continue this conversation about building a growth mindset in ourselves and promoting it in others. If you have any questions or want to share your story with me, you can write to me at vinita@techtello.com. I love to build a connection with my readers.

CONCLUSION

I can keep going

THANK YOU for taking the time to read this book and staying with me till the end. I appreciate your commitment to transform your life. I hope this book helps you see the power of a growth mindset and take steps to build it - not for days or weeks, but for a lifetime.

I want to end with a very simple question. What do you want to look back and say about your life? Do you want your life to be about doubts, labels given to you by others, goals you were too afraid to pursue, excuses that kept you away from trying, failures that defined you, mistakes that consumed and paralyzed you, or do you want it to be exciting, thrilling and fulfilling by doing everything your heart desires, putting your best effort and learning from the process?

What do you want to look back and say *"I could not..." "I did not..." "I could have been..."* or *"I tried..." "I gave my best..." "I wasn't afraid..."*

Without exercising your growth mindset you cannot make space for the things you value in life. You need to strengthen your muscles to let positive thoughts in and push negative thoughts out. Not once. Not twice. Every single day. You need to practice to reframe the not-so-good events in your life. You need to practice to act with intention instead of reacting to your circumstances. You need to practice to handle failures and setbacks to push you forward instead of pulling you back. You need to practice utilizing the power of people around you to help you think and see clearly. You need to practice self-compassion instead of raising your self-esteem. You need to practice to remind yourself about all the wonderful things you haven't achieved...YET.

Don't stop practicing your growth mindset. It will be remarkable to see the progress you can make when you don't stop working. It will be remarkable to see the skills you can build when you don't stop learning. It will be remarkable to see the goals you can achieve when you aren't afraid. It will be remarkable to see the life you can build for yourself with a simple change of beliefs.

That's the power of the growth mindset. There's no limit to what you can achieve when you value learning and effort over innate talent.

Writing this book has been one of the hardest things I have done and this book is a perfect example of me practicing what I earnestly advocate. I could have taken the easy path and skipped writing this book, but it was my growth mindset that encouraged me to embrace this challenge. Instead of telling myself "I can't," I asked, "What's the worst that can happen?" I challenged myself to build the skills required to write a book. I decided to enjoy the process instead of worrying about the outcome. I reminded myself to use the feedback from this book as information to do better next time.

If you find that I have made a mistake somewhere in this book through wrong attribution or failed to give credit where it is due, please email me at vinita@techtello.com so that I can fix the issue and thank you for helping me correct my mistake.

Finally, if you believe this book can benefit others around you, make sure to tell them about it. Please share your feedback on the platform where you purchased this book. I'd love to hear about it. Honest reviews help readers find the right book for their needs. Thanks for your support!

APPENDIX

ABOUT THE AUTHOR

Vinita Bansal has 15 years of experience in the technology space where she worked at top tech Indian startups like Flipkart and Swiggy. She has led large scale products and engineering teams of 100+ people. She has coached and mentored people from diverse backgrounds to build the skills and support required to grow in their careers and feel confident to take on higher level responsibilities within their organizations.

She founded techtello.com to help others with the skills, strategies and tools to advance in their career and succeed in their goals by reprogramming beliefs and turning obstacles into opportunities.

She is inspired by anything that helps shape her thinking, encourages her to doubt her knowledge, and guides her to continue investing in her own learning and growth. She likes to interact with people who defy conventional wisdom and challenges her to have a fresh perspective on life.

For more information, visit www.techtello.com or write to her at vinita@techtello.com.

WHAT TO READ NEXT?

It has been a pleasure sharing everything I have practiced and learnt about the growth mindset with you. I am sure you are excited about applying these concepts to your life. If you are looking for additional material, here are a few suggestions.

I have cited all the resources used in the writing of this book so that you can consult the original texts if you wish. They should serve as excellent material to go deep into a topic if something catches your attention.

If you enjoyed *Upgrade Your Mindset*, you might like my other writing as well. My free weekly newsletter covers my latest articles and other excellent resources to keep you growing. You can sign up at: techtello.com/newsletter.

Recommended Books:

Mindset: The New Psychology of Success by Carol Dweck

The Obstacle Is the Way: The Timeless Art of Turning Trials into Triumph by Ryan Holiday

Grit: The Power of Passion and Perseverance by Angela Duckworth

Rising Strong: How the Ability to Reset Transforms the Way We Live, Love, Parent, and Lead by Brene Brown

The Brain That Changes Itself: Stories of Personal Triumph from the Frontiers of Brain Science by Norman Doidge

Screw It, Let's Do It: Lessons in Life by Richard Branson

Emotional Intelligence: Why It Can Matter More Than IQ by Daniel Goleman

The Happiness Trap: How to Stop Struggling and Start Living: A Guide to ACT by Russ Harris

Man's Search for Meaning by Viktor Frankl

Atomic Habits: An Easy & Proven Way to Build Good Habits & Break Bad Ones by James Clear

Notes

INTRODUCTION

1 **Bethany Hamilton:** "Bethany Hamilton," *Wikipedia*, June 1, 2021, https://en.wikipedia.org/wiki/Bethany_Hamilton

2 **Life is a lot like surfing:** Bethany Hamilton & Rick Bundschuh & Sheryl Berk, *Soul Surfer: A True Story of Faith, Family, and Fighting to Get Back on the Board* (New York MTV Pocket, 2004)

3 **Katharine Graham:** "Katharine Graham," *Wikipedia*, May 30, 2021, https://en.wikipedia.org/wiki/Katharine_Graham; "Katharine Graham Offers Advice on Leadership," *alumni.hbs.edu*, June 1, 1998, https://www.alumni.hbs.edu/stories/Pages/story-bulletin.aspx?num=5522

4 **She was gutsy:** Steve Twomey, "A Pioneer With Courage, Influence And Humility," *Washington Post*, July 18, 2001, https://www.washingtonpost.com/archive/politics/2001/07/18/a-pioneer-with-courage-influence-and-humility/5b1aa5aa-87fa-4b7e-b494-66ffa4051ad1/

5 **I learned so much:** Neal Conan, "Chess Champion Offers Success Strategies for Life," *npr.org*, May 14, 2007, https://www.npr.org/transcripts/10170841

6 loss was ultimately: Neal Conan, "Chess Champion Offers Success Strategies for Life," *npr.org*, May 14, 2007, https://www.npr.org/transcripts/10170841

CHAPTER 1

1 **Your beliefs:** Maria Konnikova, "Hamlet and the Power of Beliefs to Shape Reality," *Scientific American*, February 18, 2012, https://blogs.scientificamerican.com/literally-psyched/hamlet-and-the-power-of-beliefs-to-shape-reality/

2 **The view you adopt for yourself:** Carol Dweck, *Mindset: Changing The Way You think To Fulfil Your Potential*, 6th ed. (London: Robinson, 2017), 5

3 **you can change them:** Wray Herbert, "How Beliefs About the Self Shape Personality and Behavior," *Psychological Science*, August 1, 2007, https://www.psychologicalscience.org/observer/how-beliefs-about-the-self-shape-personality-and-behavior

4 **Success and failure is a part of their identity:** This New York Times article mentions failure transformed from an action to an identity. Amy Waldman, "Why Nobody Likes A Loser; Failure? No, a Bump On the Road to Success," *The New York Times*, August 21, 1999, https://www.nytimes.com/1999/08/21/arts/why-nobody-likes-a-loser-failure-no-a-bump-on-the-road-to-success.html

5 **fixed mindset:** Synopsis of the fixed mindset as described by Carol Dweck in her research on mindsets. For more, see Carol Dweck, *Mindset: Changing The Way You think To Fulfil Your Potential*, 6th ed. (London: Robinson, 2017)

6 **talent is not all there is to achievement:** This part is an adaptation from the research done on Grit. For more, see Angela Duckworth, *Grit: The Power of Passion and Perseverance* (London: Vermilion, 2019)

7 **Even geniuses have to work hard:** Carol Dweck, *Mindset: Changing The Way You think To Fulfil Your Potential,* 6th ed. (London: Robinson, 2017), 41

8 **growth mindset:** Synopsis of the growth mindset as described by Carol Dweck in her research on mindsets. For more, see Carol Dweck, *Mindset: Changing The Way You think To Fulfil Your Potential,* 6th ed. (London: Robinson, 2017)

9 **false growth mindset:** Christine Gross-Loh, "How Praise Became a Consolation Prize," *The Atlantic,* December 16, 2016, https://www.theatlantic.com/education/archive/2016/12/how-praise-became-a-consolation-prize/510845/

10 **It's not just about effort:** David Scott Yeager & Carol S. Dweck, "Mindsets That Promote Resilience: When Students Believe That Personal Characteristics Can Be Developed," *Educational Psychologist*, 47 (2012), doi: 10.1080/00461520.2012.722805

11 **People can often do more:** Kira Newman, "How to Be a Lifelong Learner," *Greater Good Magazine,* April 20, 2017, https://greatergood.berkeley.edu/article/item/how_to_be_a_lifelong_learner

12 only determinant of success is our mindset: Eduardo Briceño, "Growth Mindset: Clearing up Some Common Confusions," *MindShift*, November 16, 2015, https://www.kqed.org/mindshift/42769/growth-mindset-clearing-up-some-common-confusions

13 Research shows that: Greg McKenna, "This study shows talent is overrated, and luck plays a huge role in success," *businessinsider.com.au*, Nov 22, 2018, https://www.businessinsider.com.au/this-study-shows-talent-is-overrated-as-luck-plays-a-huge-role-in-success-2018-11

14 How different our lives are: Stephen R. Covey, *The 7 Habits of Highly Effective People: Powerful Lessons in Personal Change*, 25th ed. (New York: RosettaBooks, 2013), 105

CHAPTER 2

1 **Your brain has the amazing ability:** Jesse Niebaum & Silvia Bunge, "Your Brain is Like a Muscle: Use it and Make it Strong," *Frontiers for Young Minds*, 2 (2014), doi: 10.3389/frym.2014.00005.

2 **your brain cells aren't fixed:** Ker Than, "Adults Brain Cells Do Keep Growing," *Live Science*, December 27, 2005, https://www.livescience.com/505-adult-brain-cells-growing.html

3 **You can grow your intelligence:** NAIS, "You Can Grow Your Brain," *National Association of Independent Schools*, Winter 2008, https://www.nais.org/magazine/independent-school/winter-2008/you-can-grow-your-intelligence/

4 **That's what makes it so fabulous:** Dr. Michael Merzenich, "You're Designed to Be a Learner," *Youtube*, Feb 7, 2020, https://www.youtube.com/watch?v=JRo-tXFl6c4. Here are some additional resources on this subject: Dr. Michael Merzenich, "Growing evidence of brain plasticity," *TED*, February 2004, https://www.ted.com/talks/michael_merzenich_growing_evidence_of_brain_plasticity; Dr. Michael Merzenich, *Soft-Wired: How the New Science of Brain Plasticity Can Change Your Life*, 2nd ed. (San Francisco: Parnassus Publishing, 2013); Norman Doidge, *The Brain That Changes Itself: Stories of Personal Triumph from the Frontiers of Brain Science* (New York: Penguin Books, 2007)

5 **Like sand on a beach:** Sharon Begley, "The Brain: How The Brain Rewires Itself," *Time*, January 19, 2007, http://content.time.com/time/magazine/article/0,9171,1580438-2,00.html

6 desirable difficulties: Elizabeth L. Bjork and Robert Bjork, "Making Things Hard on Yourself, but in a Good Way: Creating Desirable Difficulties to Enhance Learning," *Psychology and the Real World: Essays Illustrating Fundamental Contributions to Society*, ed. Morton A. Gernsbacher et al. (New York: Worth Publishers, 2011), 56–64

7 It is not the critic who counts: Theodore Roosevelt, "Citizenship In A Republic," *Theodore Roosevelt Center at Dickinson State University*, April 23, 1910, https://www.theodorerooseveltcenter.org/Learn-About-TR/TR-Encyclopedia/Culture-and-Society/Man-in-the-Arena.aspx

8 I'm not going to finish: Angela Duckworth, *Grit: The Power of Passion and Perseverance* (London: Vermilion, 2019), 203-205

9 I won't quit: Steven F. Maier and Martin E. Seligman, "Learned Helplessness: Theory and Evidence," Journal of Experimental Psychology 105 (1976): 3–46. See also Martin E. P. Seligman, *Learned Optimism: How to Change Your Mind and Your Life* (New York: Vintage Books, 2006)

10 You will come across obstacles: Ryan Holiday, *The Obstacle Is the Way: The Timeless Art of Turning Trials into Triumph* (New York: Portfolio/Penguin, 2014), 21

11 consistent practice of repeating strong words: Amanda Loudin, "Why athletes should treat the brain like a muscle," *Washington Post*, April 11, 2017, https://www.washingtonpost.com/lifestyle/wellness/why-athletes-should-treat-the-brain-like-a-muscle/2017/04/10/0059c41a-1966-11e7-bcc2-7d1a0973e7b2_story.html

12 **Most people don't even consider:** James Clear, *Atomic Habits: An Easy & Proven Way to Build Good Habits & Break Bad Ones* (New York: Random House, 2018), 32

13 **three layers of change:** James Clear, *Atomic Habits: An Easy & Proven Way to Build Good Habits & Break Bad Ones* (New York: Random House, 2018), 30-31

14 **Most impressions and thoughts arise:** Daniel Kahneman, *Thinking, Fast And Slow* (London: Penguin Books, 2012), 4

15 **Your unconscious mind:** What I call an unconscious and conscious mind is referred to as System 1 and System 2 by Daniel Kahneman. He states - System 1 operates automatically and quickly, with little or no effort and no sense of voluntary control. System 2 allocates attention to the effortful mental activities that demand it, including complex computations. He expands on how System 1 operates when he says "The knowledge is stored in memory and accessed without intention and without effort." For more, see Daniel Kahneman, *Thinking, Fast And Slow* (London: Penguin Books, 2012)

16 **Without your conscious awareness:** Jennifer Vrabel & Virgil Zeigler-Hill, "Conscious vs. Unconscious Determinants of Behavior", *Encyclopedia of Personality and Individual Differences*, 2017, doi: 10.1007/978-3-319-28099-8_1124-1; John Bargh & Ezequiel Morsella, "The Unconscious Mind," *Perspectives on Psychological Science*, 3 (2008), 73-79, doi: 10.1111/j.1745-6916.2008.00064.x

17 **When you get stuck:** David Rock, *Your Brain at Work: Strategies for Overcoming Distraction, Regaining Focus, and Working* (New York: HarperCollins, 2009)

18 **once depleted, it's less effective:** Amir, "Tough Choices: How Making Decisions Tires Your Brain," *Scientific American*, July 22, 2008, https://www.scientificamerican.com/article/tough-choices-how-making/

19 **One big advantage:** David Rock, *Your Brain at Work: Strategies for Overcoming Distraction, Regaining Focus, and Working* (New York: HarperCollins, 2009), 15-16

CHAPTER 3

1 **What doesn't kill me:** Friedrich Nietzsche, *The Anti-Christ, Ecce Homo, Twilight of the Idols: and Other Writings*, ed. Aaron Ridley, trans. Judith Norman (Cambridge, UK: Cambridge University Press, 2005), 157

2 **Do they encourage open discussions:** These questions are inspired by this article: Amy Edmondson, "Strategies for learning from failure," *Harvard Business Review*, April 2011, https://hbr.org/2011/04/strategies-for-learning-from-failure

3 **Success is never final:** "The Wizard's Wisdom: 'Woodenism,'" *ESPN*, June 4, 2010, https://www.espn.in/mens-college-basketball/news/story?id=5249709

4 **I had the opportunity:** James Oberg, "Shuttle manager reflects on mistakes," *NBC News*, January 28, 2004, https://www.nbcnews.com/id/wbna4086918

5 **The first thing we've got to do:** Geoff Brumfiel, "Total Failure: When The Space Shuttle Didn't Come Home," *National Public Radio*, May 17, 2017, https://www.npr.org/2017/05/17/527052122/total-failure-when-the-space-shuttle-didnt-come-home

6 **apologizing for making a mistake:** Consolidation of multiple transcripts and articles. Full list here: "CNN Larry King Live," *CNN*, January 26, 2006, http://transcripts.cnn.com/TRANSCRIPTS/0601/26/lkl.01.html; "Oprah to author: 'You conned us all,'" *CNN*, January 27, 2006, https://edition.cnn.com/2006/SHOWBIZ/books/01/27/oprah.frey/index.html; "Journalists Speak Out," *oprah.com*, January 26, 2006, https://www.oprah.com/oprahshow/journalists-speak-out/all; Edward Wyatt, "Author Is Kicked Out of Oprah Winfrey's Book Club," *New York Times*, January 27, 2006, https://www.nytimes.com/2006/01/27/books/27oprah.html; Elliot Aronson and Carol Tavris, *Mistakes Were Made (But Not By Me): Why We Justify Foolish Beliefs, Bad Decisions and Hurtful Acts*, 1st ed. (Orlando: Harcourt, 2007)

7 **In life our first job is this:** Epictetus, *Discourses and Selected Writings (Penguin Classics)*, ed. trans. Robert Dobbin (New York: Penguin, 2008), 92

8 **Failure isn't a necessary evil:** Ed Catmull and Amy Wallace, *Creativity, Inc.: Overcoming the Unseen Forces That Stand in the Way of True Inspiration* (New York: Random House, 2014), 188

9 **you wish yourself out of existence:** Paraphrased for greater clarity. Kathryn Schulz, *Being Wrong: Adventures in the Margin of Error* (New York: HarperCollins, 2010), 26

10 **lying to ourselves:** Elliot Aronson and Carol Tavris, *Mistakes Were Made (But Not By Me): Why We Justify Foolish Beliefs, Bad Decisions and Hurtful Acts*, 1st ed. (Orlando: Harcourt, 2007), 4

11 **five whys technique:** "Five whys," *Wikipedia*, February 8, 2021, https://en.wikipedia.org/wiki/Five_whys

12 **If you can admit a mistake:** Elliot Aronson and Carol Tavris, *Mistakes Were Made (But Not By Me): Why We Justify Foolish Beliefs, Bad Decisions and Hurtful Acts,* 1st ed. (Orlando: Harcourt, 2007), 221

CHAPTER 4

1 **The winners will create a long list:** Mark Gibson, "I can't yet! How to get your gymnasts excited about all the things they can't do yet," *USAGO: USA Gymnastics Magazine Online: Dealing with Fear*, reprinted from the May/June 1999, https://usagym.org/pages/home/publications/usagymnastics/1999/3/icantyet.pdf

2 **Human beings are naturally inclined:** Tom Stafford, "Why are we so curious?," *BBC*, June 19, 2012, https://www.bbc.com/future/article/20120618-why-are-we-so-curious

3 **Yet isn't the result of brazen persistence:** Seth Godin, "A simple missing word," *Seth's Blog*, February 4, 2021, https://seths.blog/2021/02/a-simple-missing-word/

4 **If you've ever picked up:** Deb Amlen, "How to Solve The New York Times Crossword," *The New York Times*, https://www.nytimes.com/guides/crosswords/how-to-solve-a-crossword-puzzle

5 **There are so many things:** Heidi Harrell, "Yet," *Groton Community School*, November 2017, https://www.grotoncommunityschool.org/wp-content/uploads/2017/11/The-Power-of-YET-Poem.pdf

6 **persist and resist:** Epictetus, *Discourses and Selected Writings (Penguin Classics)*, ed. trans. Robert Dobbin (New York: Penguin, 2008), 193

7 too stupid to learn anything: "But They Did Not Give Up," *University of Kentucky*, https://www.uky.edu/~eushe2/Pajares/OnFailingG.html

8 Between 1899 to 1905: "Inventing a flying machine," *Smithsonian National Air and Space Museum*, https://airandspace.si.edu/exhibitions/wright-brothers/online/fly/; "Wright brothers," *Wikipedia*, February 11, 2021, https://en.wikipedia.org/wiki/Wright_brothers

9 The art of flying: Shilo Brooks, "Why Did the Wright Brothers Succeed When Others Failed?," *Scientific American*, March 14, 2020, https://blogs.scientificamerican.com/observations/why-did-the-wright-brothers-succeed-when-others-failed/

10 It is the complexity of the flying: William J. Clinton, "Proclamation 6965 of December 13, 1996," *Govinfo*, January 1, 1997, https://www.govinfo.gov/content/pkg/CFR-1997-title3-vol1/html/CFR-1997-title3-vol1-proc6965.htm

11 Failure and disappointment didn't stop him: Jeff Stibel, "Michael Jordan: A Profile in Failure," August, 29, 2017, https://csq.com/2017/08/michael-jordan-profile-failure/

12 Don't be afraid to ask questions: ABC News, "Text of President Obama's School Speech," *ABC News*, September 7, 2009, https://abcnews.go.com/Politics/president-obamas-back-school-message-students/story?id=8509426

13 illusion of transparency: Thomas Gilovich, Kenneth Savitsky & Victoria Medvec, "The Illusion of Transparency: Biased Assessments of Others' Ability to Read One's Emotional States," *Journal of personality and social psychology*, 75 (1998), 332-46, doi: 10.1037//0022-3514.75.2.332

14 People are more willing to help: Marguerite Rigoglioso, "Francis Flynn: If You Want Something, Ask For It," *Stanford Graduate School of Business*, July 1, 2008, https://www.gsb.stanford.edu/insights/francis-flynn-if-you-want-something-ask-it

15 would love to get together: Compiled from interviews, articles and books. Full list here: Angela Chen, "A social psychologist explains why we should ask for help more often," *The Verge*, June 22, 2018, https://www.theverge.com/2018/6/22/17475134/heidi-grant-reinforcements-help-social-psychology; "How to become comfortable asking for help," *CBS This Morning*, August 28, 2018, https://www.youtube.com/watch?v=yXz9aoHdnnk; Heidi Grant, *Reinforcements: How to Get People to Help You* (Boston, Massachusetts: Harvard Business Review Press, 2018)

16 You are thirty times more likely: Vanessa K. Bohns, "A Face-to-Face Request Is 34 Times More Successful Than an Email," *Harvard Business Review*, April 11, 2017, https://hbr.org/2017/04/a-face-to-face-request-is-34-times-more-successful-than-an-emai

17 **exhibit intellectual humility:** Tenelle Porter, "The Benefits of Admitting When You Don't Know," *Behavioral Scientist*, April 30, 2018, https://behavioralscientist.org/the-benefits-of-admitting-when-you-dont-know/

18 **having faith in our capability:** Adam Grant, *Think Again: The Power of Knowing What You Don't Know* (New York: Viking, 2021), 46-47

19 **You can't learn:** Ryan Holiday, *Ego Is the Enemy* (New York: Portfolio, Penguin, 2016), 42

20 **treating critiques as investigations:** Mike Davidson, "How To Give Helpful Product Design Feedback," *Mike Industries (Blog)*, June 15, 2017, https://mikeindustries.com/blog/archive/2017/06/how-to-give-helpful-product-design-feedback

CHAPTER 5

1 **Without effort:** Angela Duckworth, *Grit: The Power of Passion and Perseverance* (London: Vermilion, 2019), 51-52

2 **Michael Phelps:** "Michael Phelps," *Britannica*, January 20, 2021, https://www.britannica.com/biography/Michael-Phelps

3 **You would think:** Michael Phelps, *Beneath the Surface: My Story* (New York: Sports Publishing, 2016), 16

4 **I don't want to say it's easy:** Chris Gorski, "The Science Behind Michael Phelps' Success," *Inside Science*, June 2, 2017, https://www.insidescience.org/news/science-behind-michael-phelps-success

5 **Her novel was rejected:** Jacob Shamsian, "How J.K. Rowling went from struggling single mom to the world's most successful author," *Insider*, July 31, 2018, https://www.insider.com/jk-rowling-harry-potter-author-biography-2017-7

6 **We live in a world:** Carl Honore, "In praise of slowness," *TED*, July 2005, https://www.ted.com/talks/carl_honore_in_praise_of_slowness

7 **when the tough parts:** Seth Godin, "Just the good parts," *Seth's Blog*, March 31, 2013, https://seths.blog/2013/03/just-the-good-parts/

8 **It was beautiful:** Steve Jobs, "'You've got to find what you love,' Jobs says," *Stanford News*, June 14, 2005, https://news.stanford.edu/2005/06/14/jobs-061505/

9 **Technology alone is not enough:** Jonah Lehrer, "Steve Jobs: "Technology Alone Is Not Enough"," *The New Yorker*, October 7, 2011, https://www.newyorker.com/news/news-desk/steve-jobs-technology-alone-is-not-enough

10 **using AI on satellite data:** Michael Chui, Martin Harrysson, James Manyika, Roger Roberts, Rita Chung, Pieter Nel, and Ashley van Heteren, "Applying artificial intelligence for social good," *McKinsey Global Institute*, November 28, 2018, https://www.mckinsey.com/featured-insights/artificial-intelligence/applying-artificial-intelligence-for-social-good

11 **Increasing specialization has created a system:** David Epstein, Range: Why Generalists Triumph in a Specialized World (New York: Riverhead Books, 2019), 12, 29, 47

12 **We are A-to-Z thinkers:** Ryan Holiday, *The Obstacle Is the Way: The Timeless Art of Turning Trials into Triumph* (New York: Portfolio/Penguin, 2014), 76

13 **Radical change is like charging:** Robert Maurer, *One Small Step Can Change Your Life: The Kaizen Wa*y (New York: Workman, 2004), 15-16

14 **taking small steps:** "Kaizen," *Wikipedia*, March 2, 2021, https://en.wikipedia.org/wiki/Kaizen

15 **One cannot enjoy doing the same thing:** Mihaly Csikszentmihalyi, *Flow: The Psychology of Happiness* (London: Ebury Publishing, 2013), 75

16 **Enjoyment appears at the boundary:** Mihaly Csikszentmihalyi, *Flow: The Psychology of Happiness* (London: Ebury Publishing, 2013), 52

17 **Goldilocks rule:** "Goldilocks principle," *Wikipedia*, February 3, 2021, https://en.wikipedia.org/wiki/Goldilocks_principle

18 **In one experiment:** Peter Gollwitzer, "Implementation Intentions: Strong Effects of Simple Plans," *American Psychologist*, 54 (1999), 493-503, doi: 10.1037/0003-066X.54.7.493

19 **researchers in Great Britain:** Sarah Milne, Sheina Orbell & Paschal Sheeran, "Combining motivational and volitional interventions to promote exercise participation: Protection motivation theory and implementation intentions," *British journal of health psychology*, 7 (2002), 163-84, doi: 10.1348/135910702169420

CHAPTER 6

1 **It's our overall sense of self-worth:** "Self-esteem," *Wikipedia*, March 10, 2021, https://en.wikipedia.org/wiki/Self-esteem

2 **Hans Christain Anderson's story:** "The Emperor's New Clothes," *The Hans Christian Andersen Center,* September 19, 2019, https://andersen.sdu.dk/vaerk/hersholt/TheEmperorsNewClothes_e.html

3 **We grasp onto self-esteem:** Kristin Neff, *Self Compassion* (London: Hodder and Stoughton, 2011), 151-152

4 **I started to see clearly:** Mandy Stadtmiller, "How I Stopped Sitting Around All Day Seething With Jealousy of My Peers," *medium.com*, April 8, 2019, https://humanparts.medium.com/why-is-everyone-succeeding-but-me-29186494166b

5 **As long as you view the people:** Amy Morin, *13 Things Mentally Strong People Don't Do,* 1st ed. (New York: William Morrow, 2014), 141

6 **Attempt to create positive self-esteem:** *Principles of Social Psychology - 1st International Edition* (Vancouver: BCcampus OpenEd, Minneapolis: Open Textbook Library, 2014)

7 **You can make mistakes:** Jon Mertz, "John Wooden: A Principled Life," *ThinDifference.com*, June 5, 2010, https://www.thindifference.com/2010/06/john-wooden-a-principled-life/

8 **Failure is where success:** Scott Adams, *How to Fail at Almost Everything and Still Win Big: Kind of the Story of My Life* (New York: Portfolio/Penguin, 2013), 16

9 **discouraged and depressed:** Theodore Powers & Richard Koestner & David Zuroff, "Self–Criticism, Goal Motivation, and Goal Progress," *Journal of Social and Clinical Psychology*, 26 (2007), 826-840, doi: 10.1521/jscp.2007.26.7.826; Sidney J. Blatt, "Dependency and Self-Criticism: Psychological Dimensions of Depression," *Journal of Consulting and Clinical Psychology*, 50 (1982), 113–24, doi: 10.1037/0022-006X.50.1.113

10 **Babies don't hold the same tendency:** Paraphrased for greater clarity. Original quote by Dan Millman "If babies held the same tendency toward self-criticism as adults, they might never learn to walk or talk. Can you imagine infants stomping, 'Aarggh! Screwed up again!' Fortunately, babies are free of self-criticism. They just keep practicing."

11 **high self-esteem does not predict:** Roy Baumeister & Jennifer Campbell & Joachim Krueger & Kathleen Vohs, "Does High Self-Esteem Cause Better Performance, Interpersonal Success, Happiness, or Healthier Lifestyles?," *Psychological Science in the Public Interest*, 4 (2003), 1-44, doi: 10.1111/1529-1006.01431

12 **Instead of mercilessly judging:** Dr. Kristin Neff, *self-compassion.org*, https://self-compassion.org/the-three-elements-of-self-compassion-2/

13 **Many studies show:** Ricks Warren & Elke Smeets & Kristin Neff, "Self-criticism and self-compassion: Risk and resilience: Being compassionate to oneself is associated with emotional resilience and psychological well-being," *self-compassion.org*, December 2016, https://self-compassion.org/wp-content/uploads/2016/12/Self-Criticism.pdf; Kristin Neff & Stephanie Rude & Kristin Kirkpatrick, "An examination of self-compassion in relation to positive psychological functioning and personality traits," *Journal of Research in Personality*, 41 (2007), 908-916, doi: 10.1016/j.jrp.2006.08.002

14 **The biggest misconception:** Kristin Neff, "The Five Myths of Self-Compassion," *Greater Good Science Center*, September 30, 2015, https://greatergood.berkeley.edu/article/item/the_five_myths_of_self_compassion

15 **Research also shows:** Sara Dunne & David Sheffield & Joseph Chilcot, "Brief report: Self-compassion, physical health and the mediating role of health-promoting behaviours," *Journal of health psychology*, 23 (2016), doi: 10.1177/1359105316643377

16 **Self-compassion provides the intrinsic motivation:** Juliana Breines & Serena Chen, "Self-Compassion Increases Self-Improvement Motivation," *Personality & social psychology bulletin*, 38 (2012), 1133-43, doi: 10.1177/0146167212445599

17 **exercises on her website:** Kristin Neff, "Self-Compassion Guided Meditations and Exercises," *self-compassion.org*, https://self-compassion.org/category/exercises/#exercises

CHAPTER 7

1 **Goals are good for planning:** James Clear, "Forget About Setting Goals. Focus on This Instead," *jamesclear.com*, https://jamesclear.com/goals-systems

2 **We respond strongly to the cues:** Siegwart Lindenberg, How cues in the environment affect normative behavior, *Environmental Psychology: An Introduction* (2012), 119-128

3 **Successful people don't wish:** Scott Adams, *How to Fail at Almost Everything and Still Win Big: Kind of the Story of My Life* (New York: Portfolio/Penguin, 2013), 46

4 **The power of knowing:** Pete Carroll, "How your personal philosophy leads to perseverance in uncertain times," *competetocreate.net*, July 16, 2020, https://competetocreate.net/living-by-your-philosophy/

5 **Who you are is defined by the values:** Mark Manson, "The Most Important Question of Your Life," *markmanson.net*, https://markmanson.net/question

6 **Self-Determination theory:** Edward L. Deci and Richard M. Ryan, "Facilitating Optimal Motivation and Psychological Well-Being Across Life's Domains," Canadian Psychology 49 (2008): 14-23, doi: 10.1037/0708-5591.49.1.14

7 **autonomously motivated goals:** Ken M. Sheldon, "Becoming Oneself: The Central Role of Self-Concordant Goal Selection," *Personality and Social Psychology Review*, 18 (2014), 349 - 65, doi: 10.1177/1088868314538549

8 those who wrote their goals: Gail Matthews, "Goals Research Summary," *dominican.edu*, February 2020, https://www.dominican.edu/sites/default/files/2020-02/gailmatthews-harvard-goals-researchsummary.pdf

9 People with clear, written goals: Brian Tracy, "The Law of Clarity," *briantracy.com*, https://www.briantracy.com/blog/leadership-success/the-law-of-clarity/

10 sit down with your fears: Tim Ferriss, "Fear-Setting: The Most Valuable Exercise I Do Every Month," *tim.blog*, May 15, 2017, https://tim.blog/2017/05/15/fear-setting/

11 fear setting template: Tim Ferriss, "TED_Ferriss_Fear_Setting_Sample_Slides," *tim.blog,* June 2017, https://tim.blog/wp-content/uploads/2017/06/ted_ferriss_fear_setting_sample_slides.pdf

12 goals in a goal hierarchy: Angela Duckworth & James Gross, "Self-Control and Grit: Related but Separable Determinants of Success," *Current Directions in Psychological Science*, 23 (2014), 319-325, doi: 10.1177/0963721414541462

13 Set specific and challenging goals: Edwin Locke & Gary Latham, "Building a practically useful theory of goal setting and task motivation. A 35-year odyssey," *The American psychologist*, 57 (2002), 705-17, doi: 10.1037//0003-066x.57.9.705

14 **Simpleology system called backward planning:** Ibnu Wahyudi, "Simplexology 101: The Simple Science of Getting What You Want," *academia.edu*, https://www.academia.edu/9630929/Simplexology_101_The_Simple_Science_of_Getting_What_You_Want

MINDSET TRACKER

1 habit compound over time: James Clear states "Daily habits are powerful because of how they compound, but worrying too much about every daily choice is like looking at yourself in the mirror from an inch away. You can see every imperfection and lose sight of the bigger picture. There is too much feedback. Conversely, never reviewing your habits is like never looking in the mirror. You aren't aware of easily fixable flaws—a spot on your shirt, a bit of food in your teeth. There is too little feedback. Periodic reflection and review is like viewing yourself in the mirror from a conversational distance. You can see the important changes you should make without losing sight of the bigger picture. You want to view the entire mountain range, not obsess over each peak and valley." For more, see James Clear, *Atomic Habits*: *An Easy & Proven Way to Build Good Habits & Break Bad Ones* (New York: Random House, 2018), 246-247

2 if you do something small repeatedly: Leo Babauta, "The Power of Habit Investments," *Zen Habits*, January 28, 2013, https://zenhabits.net/bank

3 moments of self reflection: Jennifer Porter, "Why You Should Make Time for Self-Reflection," *Harvard Business Review*, March 21, 2017, https://hbr.org/2017/03/why-you-should-make-time-for-self-reflection-even-if-you-hate-doing-it

PROMOTING GROWTH MINDSET IN KIDS

1 **children's health and overall development:** Leah Shafer & Bari Walsh, "Growth Mindset and Children's Health," *gse.harvard.edu*, March 15, 2017, https://www.gse.harvard.edu/news/uk/17/03/growth-mindset-and-childrens-health

2 **higher achievement in students:** "Dr. Dweck's research into growth mindset changed education forever," *mindsetworks.com*, https://www.mindsetworks.com/science/

3 **better math grades:** "The evidence: how a growth mindset leads to higher achievement," *mindsetkit.org*, https://www.mindsetkit.org/topics/about-growth-mindset/evidence-how-growth-mindset-leads-to-higher-achievement

Copyright © 2021 Vinita Bansal

All rights reserved. No part of this book may be reproduced or used in any manner without the prior written permission of the copyright owner, except for the use of brief quotations in a book review.

To request permissions, contact the publisher at vinita@techtello.com.

First Edition

www.techtello.com

Printed in France by Amazon
Brétigny-sur-Orge, FR

13852191R00150